STANLEY S GARRETT

EMINEM: THE VOICE OF A GENERATION

Impact, Influence, and Cultural Significance Updated Version 2024

Copyright © 2024 by STANLEY S GARRETT

All rights reserved. No part of this publication may be reproduced, stored or transmitted in any form or by any means, electronic, mechanical, photocopying, recording, scanning, or otherwise without written permission from the publisher. It is illegal to copy this book, post it to a website, or distribute it by any other means without permission.

First edition

This book was professionally typeset on Reedsy.
Find out more at reedsy.com

Contents

Introduction	1
1 CHAPTER 1	11
2 CHAPTER 2	20
3 CHAPTER 3	29
4 CHAPTER 4	39
5 CHAPTER 5	49
6 CHAPTER 6	59
7 CHAPTER 7	69
8 CHAPTER 8	79
9 CHAPTER 9	89
10 CHAPTER 10	99
11 CHAPTER 11	109
12 CHAPTER 12	119
13 CHAPTER 13	129
14 CHAPTER 14	139
15 Conclusion	148
Afterword	158

Introduction

In the wells of music history, few names resonate with the same intensity and controversy as Marshall Bruce Mathers III, known globally as Eminem. The Detroit-born rapper has carved out a legacy that transcends the boundaries of hip-hop, leaving an indelible mark on popular culture. His journey from the impoverished streets of Detroit to the pinnacle of global stardom is a testament to raw talent, relentless determination, and an unyielding commitment to authenticity.

Eminem's rise to fame in the late 1990s marked a seismic shift in the hip-hop landscape. His razor-sharp lyricism, coupled with a provocative persona and unfiltered storytelling, captivated audiences and polarized critics. The rapper's ability to weave complex rhyme schemes with biting social commentary and deeply personal narratives set him apart in a genre already teeming with talented wordsmiths.

The impact of Eminem's music extends far beyond record sales and chart positions. His work has sparked heated debates on freedom of expression, pushed the boundaries of acceptable content in mainstream media, and challenged societal norms. Through his alter ego, Slim Shady, Eminem created a conduit for expressing his darkest thoughts and most controversial ideas, often blurring the lines between art and reality.

Eminem's influence on the rap genre cannot be overstated. He shattered racial barriers, becoming one of the first white rappers to gain widespread respect and acclaim in a predominantly African American art form. His success paved the way for a new generation of artists who dared to defy traditional genre expectations.

The rapper's personal life has been as tumultuous and headline-grabbing as his professional career. His troubled relationship with his mother, his turbulent marriage to Kim Scott, and his struggles with addiction have all been laid bare in his lyrics, creating a deeply personal connection with his audience. Eminem's willingness to confront his demons publicly has made him a polarizing figure, admired for his honesty while simultaneously criticized for his often-graphic depictions of violence and misogyny.

Throughout his career, Eminem has demonstrated an remarkable ability to evolve artistically while maintaining his core identity. From the raw, unfiltered rage of "The Slim Shady LP" to the introspective maturity of later works like "Recovery," he has continually pushed himself creatively, exploring new themes and refining his craft.

Eminem's impact extends beyond his own discography. Through his record label, Shady Records, he has fostered the careers of numerous artists, including 50 Cent, D12, and Obie Trice. His production work and collaborations have further cemented his status as a versatile and influential figure in the music industry.

The rapper's forays into other media, most notably his semi-autobiographical film "8 Mile," have further expanded his cultural footprint. The movie's success, coupled with the Academy Award-winning song "Lose Yourself," showcased Eminem's crossover appeal and his ability to connect with audiences beyond the realm of hip-hop.

INTRODUCTION

Eminem's career has been marked by numerous accolades and record-breaking achievements. He has won multiple Grammy Awards, sold millions of albums worldwide, and consistently topped charts with each new release. His ability to remain relevant in an ever-changing music landscape is a testament to his enduring appeal and artistic vision.

The controversies surrounding Eminem have been an integral part of his public persona. His lyrics have drawn criticism from various quarters, including LGBTQ+ advocacy groups, women's rights organizations, and conservative political figures. The rapper's unapologetic stance in the face of such criticism has only served to fuel his reputation as a rebellious and uncompromising artist.

Eminem's influence on language and popular culture is profound. His clever wordplay, rapid-fire delivery, and penchant for pop culture references have seeped into the vernacular of multiple generations. Phrases coined in his lyrics have entered common usage, and his impact on the English language has been the subject of academic study.

The rapper's relationship with fame has been complex and often fraught. His lyrics frequently explore the darker side of celebrity, touching on themes of isolation, paranoia, and the pressure of public scrutiny. This introspective approach to stardom has resonated with fans and fellow artists alike, offering a raw and unvarnished look at the realities of life in the spotlight.

Eminem's musical style has evolved significantly over the course of his career. While his early work was characterized by its shock value and confrontational tone, later albums have seen him exploring more mature themes and experimenting with different production styles. This evolution has allowed him to maintain his relevance in a rapidly changing musical landscape while staying true to his artistic vision.

The rapper's influence on hip-hop production techniques is often overlooked but equally significant. His collaborations with producers like Dr. Dre have resulted in a distinctive sound that has been widely imitated. Eminem's own production work, both for himself and other artists, has further showcased his musical versatility and deep understanding of the genre.

Eminem's lyrical content has often been autobiographical, providing listeners with intimate glimpses into his personal life. From his challenging childhood and struggles with poverty to his battles with addiction and family drama, the rapper has used his music as a form of therapy, working through his issues in front of a global audience. This raw honesty has endeared him to millions of fans who see their own struggles reflected in his words.

The rapper's relationship with Detroit, his hometown, has been a recurring theme throughout his career. Eminem has never shied away from depicting the harsh realities of life in the city, but he has also consistently shown pride in his roots. His success has made him a hometown hero, and he has given back to the community through various charitable initiatives.

Eminem's impact on the business side of the music industry is also noteworthy. His success helped to revitalize Interscope Records and played a significant role in establishing Aftermath Entertainment as a powerhouse label. The rapper's savvy business moves, including the launch of Shady Records and various brand partnerships, have set a template for artists seeking to maintain control over their careers and expand their influence beyond music.

INTRODUCTION

The global reach of Eminem's music is a testament to the universal appeal of his storytelling. Despite the specifically American context of much of his work, he has found fans in every corner of the world. His concerts draw massive crowds internationally, and his albums consistently top charts in numerous countries.

Eminem's legacy in hip-hop is secure, but his influence extends far beyond the genre. He has been cited as an inspiration by artists across various musical styles, from pop to rock to country. His success has opened doors for a diverse range of voices in popular music, challenging preconceptions about who can succeed in hip-hop and what the genre can encompass.

The rapper's technical skills have set a new standard in hip-hop. His complex rhyme schemes, masterful use of alliteration and assonance, and ability to bend words to fit his rhythms have been widely studied and emulated. Eminem's influence can be heard in the work of countless rappers who have followed in his wake, all striving to match his lyrical dexterity.

Eminem's career has not been without its low points. He has faced periods of critical backlash, commercial disappointments, and personal setbacks. However, his ability to bounce back from these challenges has become a central part of his narrative. Each comeback has been met with renewed interest from fans and critics alike, eager to see how the rapper has evolved and what he has to say.

The cultural impact of Eminem's work extends to academia, where his lyrics have been the subject of serious scholarly analysis. His use of language, his exploration of identity, and his commentary on American society have all been examined in depth by researchers in fields ranging from linguistics to sociology to cultural studies.

Eminem's relationship with other artists in the hip-hop community has been complex and often contentious. His feuds with other rappers have become the stuff of legend, often playing out in diss tracks that showcase his sharp wit and verbal agility. However, he has also fostered numerous collaborative relationships, working with a wide range of artists across multiple genres.

The rapper's influence on fashion and style should not be overlooked. His signature look – bleached blonde hair, white tank top, and baggy jeans – became iconic in the early 2000s. While his personal style has evolved over the years, his impact on hip-hop fashion and youth culture remains significant.

Eminem's music has often served as a barometer for social issues in America. His willingness to tackle controversial topics head-on has made him a lightning rod for criticism but has also positioned him as an important voice in ongoing cultural debates. From discussions about race relations to explorations of class divides, his work provides a raw and unfiltered perspective on American life.

The evolution of Eminem's public persona over the course of his career offers fascinating insights into the nature of fame and identity in the modern era. From the outrageous antics of his early years to the more reserved and introspective figure he has become, the rapper's journey reflects broader changes in celebrity culture and public expectations of artists.

Eminem's enduring popularity is a testament to his ability to connect with audiences on a deep emotional level. His music has provided

INTRODUCTION

solace and inspiration to millions of fans, many of whom see their own struggles and triumphs reflected in his lyrics. This emotional resonance has created a loyal fan base that has stayed with him through the ups and downs of his career.

The technical aspects of Eminem's rapping style have been widely analyzed and praised. His ability to manipulate rhythm and flow, coupled with his expansive vocabulary and clever wordplay, has set a new standard in hip-hop lyricism. Many consider him one of the greatest technical rappers of all time, with his influence evident in the work of countless artists who have followed in his wake.

Eminem's collaborations with other artists have produced some of the most memorable moments in his discography. His work with Dr. Dre, in particular, has yielded numerous hits and helped to shape the sound of modern hip-hop. These collaborations have also allowed Eminem to showcase his versatility, adapting his style to complement a wide range of musical partners.

The rapper's ventures outside of music have further cemented his status as a cultural icon. His semi-autobiographical film "8 Mile" was a critical and commercial success, earning him an Academy Award for Best Original Song. This crossover into film demonstrated Eminem's ability to translate his artistic vision to different mediums.

Eminem's influence on popular culture extends beyond music and into the realm of language itself. His clever turns of phrase and vivid imagery have entered the lexicon, with many of his lyrics becoming popular catchphrases. This linguistic impact underscores the depth of his cultural penetration and the lasting power of his art.

The rapper's relationship with controversy has been a defining aspect of his career. His willingness to push boundaries and challenge societal norms has made him a polarizing figure, simultaneously praised for his boldness and criticized for his provocative content. This tension between artistic expression and social responsibility has been a recurring theme in discussions of his work.

Eminem's impact on the business side of the music industry is significant. His success helped to revitalize Interscope Records and played a crucial role in establishing Aftermath Entertainment as a major force in hip-hop. The launch of his own label, Shady Records, further demonstrated his business acumen and his commitment to fostering new talent.

The global reach of Eminem's music is a testament to the universal themes he explores in his work. Despite the specifically American context of many of his lyrics, he has found a devoted audience in countries around the world. This international appeal speaks to the power of his storytelling and the relatability of his personal struggles.

Eminem's willingness to address his own flaws and mistakes in his music has been a key factor in his enduring appeal. His lyrics often serve as a form of public self-examination, allowing listeners to witness his personal growth and struggles in real-time. This vulnerability has created a strong emotional connection with his audience.

The rapper's influence on hip-hop extends beyond his own music to the artists he has mentored and promoted through Shady Records. By providing a platform for talents like 50 Cent, D12, and Obie Trice, Eminem has played a crucial role in shaping the sound of contemporary hip-hop.

INTRODUCTION

Eminem's artistic evolution over the course of his career offers insights into the maturation of hip-hop as a genre. From the raw aggression of his early work to the more introspective tone of his later albums, his discography charts the growth of both the artist and the art form.

The rapper's struggles with addiction and subsequent recovery have been well-documented in his music. His willingness to confront these issues publicly has not only provided compelling material for his art but has also helped to destigmatize discussions of mental health and substance abuse in the hip-hop community.

Eminem's complex relationship with his hometown of Detroit has been a recurring theme in his work. His lyrics often paint a gritty, unromanticized picture of life in the city, while simultaneously expressing deep pride in his roots. This connection to place has been an important aspect of his artistic identity.

The critical reception of Eminem's work has varied widely over the course of his career. While he has received numerous accolades and is widely regarded as one of the greatest rappers of all time, he has also faced periods of backlash and criticism. This fluctuating critical consensus reflects the controversial nature of his art and his ability to remain a topic of discussion in the music world.

Eminem's impact on race relations in hip-hop and popular culture at large is complex and multifaceted. As a white artist who achieved unprecedented success in a predominantly black genre, he has been both praised for breaking down racial barriers and criticized for appropriating black culture. This tension has sparked important conversations about race, authenticity, and cultural exchange in music.

The rapper's lyrical content has often been the subject of intense scrutiny and debate. His graphic depictions of violence, his use of homophobic and misogynistic language, and his dark humor have all drawn criticism from various quarters. These controversies have raised important questions about artistic freedom, social responsibility, and the power of words.

Eminem's influence can be seen in the work of numerous artists across multiple genres. His technical skill, storytelling ability, and willingness to tackle difficult subjects have inspired a generation of musicians to push the boundaries of their art. This far-reaching impact cements his status as one of the most influential artists of his generation.

CHAPTER 1

The Making of Marshall Mathers

1.1 Birth and Early Childhood in Saint Joseph, Missouri

Marshall Bruce Mathers III entered the world on October 17, 1972, in St. Joseph, Missouri. His birth marked the beginning of a tumultuous journey that would eventually lead to global stardom. Born to Deborah Rae Nelson and Marshall Bruce Mathers Jr., young Marshall's early years were fraught with instability and hardship.

The circumstances surrounding Marshall's birth were far from ideal. His mother, Deborah, was merely 15 years old when she gave birth to him after a brief relationship with his father. The young couple's marriage lasted only a few months, with Marshall Sr. abandoning the family when his son was just an infant. This early absence of a father figure would have a profound impact on Marshall's life and later become a recurring theme in his music.

Growing up in St. Joseph, a small city along the Missouri River, Marshall's childhood was marked by financial struggles and frequent moves. Deborah, still a teenager herself, struggled to provide for her young son. The family often relied on welfare and the support of relatives to make ends meet. These early experiences of poverty and instability would later fuel Marshall's drive to succeed and inform his gritty, realistic depictions of working-class life in his music.

Marshall's relationship with his mother was complex from the start. Deborah, dealing with her own personal issues and the challenges of young motherhood, often found it difficult to provide the stability and nurturing environment her son needed. This tumultuous mother-son dynamic would become a central theme in Marshall's future lyrics, with songs like "Cleaning Out My Closet" offering raw, unflinching portrayals of their troubled relationship.

The young Marshall showed early signs of creativity and a love for storytelling. Even as a child, he was drawn to words and their power to express emotions and ideas. He would spend hours poring over comic books and dictionaries, expanding his vocabulary and developing the linguistic dexterity that would later become his trademark as a rapper.

Marshall's early years in St. Joseph were also marked by frequent bullying and social isolation. A shy and often sickly child, he struggled to fit in with his peers. This sense of being an outsider would later fuel his alter ego, Slim Shady, and inform the confrontational, defiant stance he would adopt in his music.

The racial dynamics of St. Joseph, a predominantly white city, played a significant role in shaping Marshall's early experiences. Growing up in a working-class neighborhood, he was exposed to African American culture and music from a young age. This early immersion in hip-hop culture would prove instrumental in his future career, as he navigated the complexities of being a white artist in a predominantly black genre.

Marshall's time in St. Joseph was characterized by constant upheaval. The family moved frequently, often staying with relatives or in low-income housing. This nomadic lifestyle made it difficult for young Marshall to form lasting friendships or develop a sense of stability. However, it also fostered in him a resilience and adaptability that would serve him well in the face of future challenges.

The economic realities of life in St. Joseph in the 1970s and early 1980s provided the backdrop for Marshall's childhood. The city, like many in the Midwest, was grappling with industrial decline and economic uncertainty. These harsh realities would later inform Marshall's unflinching portrayals of working-class struggle in his music.

1.2 Move to Detroit and Schooling Challenges

The Mathers family's relocation to Detroit, Michigan, when Marshall was 11 years old, marked a pivotal moment in his life. This move from the relative quiet of St. Joseph to the gritty urban landscape of Detroit would profoundly shape his worldview and artistic sensibilities. Detroit, with its rich musical heritage and stark socioeconomic contrasts, provided the perfect backdrop for Marshall's burgeoning creativity and growing sense of alienation.

Upon arriving in Detroit, the family settled in a working-class neighborhood on the east side of the city. The stark difference between this new urban environment and the smaller city life of St. Joseph was immediately apparent. Detroit's reputation as a tough, unforgiving city was not lost on young Marshall, who found himself thrust into a world of heightened racial tensions, economic struggles, and street-level realities.

Marshall's educational journey in Detroit was fraught with challenges. The constant moving that had characterized his early years continued, resulting in frequent changes of schools. This perpetual state of being the "new kid" made it difficult for Marshall to form lasting friendships or find a sense of belonging within the school system. He attended Lincoln High School in Warren, a suburb of Detroit, but his academic career was marked by truancy, poor grades, and a general disinterest in traditional education.

The school environment proved to be a battleground for Marshall. His status as an outsider, compounded by his small stature and bleached blonde hair, made him a target for bullies. Incidents of physical confrontation were not uncommon, with Marshall often finding himself on the receiving end of violence. These experiences of alienation and victimization would later fuel the angry, defiant persona he would adopt as Eminem.

Despite his struggles in the formal education system, Marshall displayed a keen intelligence and a particular aptitude for language arts. His English teachers, while often frustrated by his behavior and lack of engagement with other subjects, recognized his talent for wordplay and creative writing. This natural affinity for language would prove to be the foundation upon which he would build his rap career.

The socioeconomic realities of Detroit in the 1980s played a significant role in shaping Marshall's worldview. The city was grappling with the

CHAPTER 1

effects of deindustrialization, white flight, and urban decay. The once-thriving Motor City was now characterized by high unemployment rates, crime, and a sense of abandonment. These harsh realities provided ample material for Marshall's future lyrics, which would often touch on themes of poverty, violence, and the struggle for survival in urban America.

Marshall's home life during this period remained unstable. His mother's erratic behavior and struggles with substance abuse created a chaotic environment that was not conducive to academic success or emotional well-being. The family continued to move frequently, often staying with relatives or in low-income housing. This lack of stability further compounded Marshall's difficulties in school and his ability to form lasting relationships with peers.

The racial dynamics of Detroit's public schools in the 1980s also played a significant role in Marshall's experiences. As a white student in predominantly African American schools, he found himself navigating complex racial tensions and cultural differences. These experiences would later inform his understanding of race relations and his unique position as a white artist in the predominantly black world of hip-hop.

Marshall's struggles with traditional education led him to seek alternative forms of self-expression. It was during this period that he began to seriously explore his interest in hip-hop, using it as an outlet for his frustrations and a means of asserting his identity. The vibrant hip-hop scene in Detroit provided ample inspiration and opportunities for a young, aspiring rapper.

By the age of 14, Marshall had largely disengaged from the formal education system. He dropped out of Lincoln High School after failing the ninth grade three times. This decision, while seemingly detrimental, allowed him to focus more intensely on developing his skills as a rapper. The streets of Detroit became his new classroom, with the city's rich musical heritage and thriving underground hip-hop scene serving as his curriculum.

1.3 Early Interest in Rap and Words

Marshall Mathers' fascination with words and language manifested early in his life, laying the groundwork for his future career as one of the most lyrically innovative rappers in the history of hip-hop. This interest, nurtured by hours spent poring over dictionaries and comic books, would evolve into a passion for rap music that would define his teenage years and shape his destiny.

The young Marshall's love affair with hip-hop began in earnest when he was introduced to the genre through his uncle Ronnie. It was Ronnie who gifted Marshall his first rap album, a copy of Ice-T's "Reckless." This moment of musical revelation opened up a new world for Marshall, exposing him to a form of expression that resonated deeply with his own experiences and emotions.

Marshall's early forays into rap were characterized by an intense dedication to honing his craft. He would spend countless hours writing rhymes, filling notebook after notebook with lyrics that reflected his inner turmoil, frustrations, and dreams. This relentless pursuit of lyrical perfection would become a hallmark of his career, setting him apart from his peers with his intricate rhyme schemes and clever wordplay.

The influence of early rap pioneers on Marshall's developing style cannot be overstated. He studied the works of artists like Rakim, Big Daddy Kane, and Kool G Rap with an almost scholarly intensity, dissecting their rhyme patterns and flow techniques. This deep immersion in the art form allowed him to develop a unique style that combined technical proficiency with raw emotional honesty.

Marshall's early rapping was not confined to the privacy of his bedroom. He began participating in local rap battles and open mic nights, testing his skills against other aspiring MCs in Detroit's burgeoning hip-hop scene. These experiences, often challenging and sometimes humiliating, served to sharpen his skills and develop the thick skin necessary to succeed in the competitive world of rap.

The racial dynamics of Detroit's hip-hop scene presented unique challenges for the young Marshall. As a white rapper in a predominantly black genre, he faced skepticism and outright hostility from some quarters. However, his undeniable skill and passion for the art form gradually earned him respect among his peers, regardless of race.

Marshall's lyrical content during this early period reflected his tumultuous personal life and the harsh realities of his environment. His rhymes were often dark, angry, and filled with vivid depictions of violence and drug use. This raw, unfiltered approach to songwriting would become a defining characteristic of his later work as Eminem.

The formation of Marshall's alter ego, Slim Shady, can be traced back to this formative period. Slim Shady emerged as a way for Marshall to express his most outrageous and controversial thoughts, serving as a kind of lyrical id that allowed him to push the boundaries of acceptable content in his rhymes.

Marshall's dedication to his craft often came at the expense of other aspects of his life. His academic performance suffered as he focused more and more on developing his rap skills. This single-minded pursuit of his passion would eventually lead him to drop out of school, a decision that, while risky, allowed him to devote himself fully to his music.

The influence of Detroit's rich musical heritage on Marshall's developing style was significant. The city's legacy of Motown, rock, and hip-hop provided a diverse sonic palette from which he could draw inspiration. This eclectic musical background would later manifest in his willingness to experiment with different genres and production styles in his music.

Marshall's early attempts at recording were humble affairs, often taking place in makeshift home studios with borrowed or secondhand equipment. These early demos, while rough and unpolished, showcased his raw talent and unique voice, catching the attention of local producers and fellow artists.

The young rapper's growing reputation in Detroit's underground scene led to his first real break when he was invited to join the rap group New Jacks. While this collaboration was short-lived, it provided Marshall with valuable experience and exposure, further fueling his determination to succeed in the music industry.

Marshall's lyrics during this period often touched on themes of escape and aspiration. Growing up in poverty and instability, he saw rap as his ticket out of his difficult circumstances. This dream of using his words to change his life would become a driving force in his pursuit of a music career.

CHAPTER 1

The development of Marshall's rapid-fire delivery and complex rhyme schemes can be traced back to these early years of practice and experimentation. He would spend hours perfecting his timing and flow, developing the technical skills that would later set him apart in the world of professional rap.

Marshall's early interest in words extended beyond just rap lyrics. He was an avid reader, often losing himself in books as a way to escape his difficult reality. This love of literature would later manifest in the literary and pop culture references that pepper his lyrics, adding layers of meaning to his songs.

The young rapper's growing skill and local fame began to attract attention from small record labels and producers in the Detroit area. While these early opportunities didn't lead to immediate success, they provided valuable learning experiences and helped to refine his understanding of the music industry.

Marshall's commitment to authenticity in his lyrics was evident from the start. He refused to adopt a fake 'gangsta' persona, instead choosing to rap about his own experiences and emotions, no matter how painful or embarrassing. This honesty would become a hallmark of his later work, endearing him to millions of fans who saw their own struggles reflected in his music.

2

CHAPTER 2

Rise of Slim Shady

2.1 Participation in the Detroit Rap Scene

Marshall Mathers' immersion in the Detroit rap scene marked a crucial turning point in his journey towards becoming Eminem. The city's vibrant hip-hop culture provided the perfect crucible for his raw talent to be forged into something truly extraordinary.

Detroit's rap scene in the 1990s was a fiercely competitive arena, teeming with aspiring artists all vying for recognition. Marshall threw himself into this world with unbridled passion and determination. He frequented local clubs and underground venues, participating in rap battles that would become the stuff of legend.

The Hip Hop Shop on 7 Mile Road became a second home to Marshall. This iconic venue hosted weekly open mic contests where he honed his skills, facing off against some of Detroit's most talented MCs. These battles were more than just competitions; they were rigorous training grounds where Marshall learned to think on his feet, crafting razor-sharp rhymes in real-time.

Marshall's performances at these events quickly garnered attention. His rapid-fire delivery, intricate wordplay, and fearless attitude set him apart from his peers. Even in defeat, he displayed a resilience and hunger that impressed both fellow rappers and audiences alike.

The racial dynamics of Detroit's hip-hop scene presented unique challenges for Marshall. As a white rapper in a predominantly black genre, he initially faced skepticism and outright hostility. However, his undeniable skill and genuine passion for the art form gradually earned him respect among his peers.

Marshall's participation in the Detroit rap scene went beyond just battling. He began collaborating with other local artists, forming connections that would prove invaluable in his future career. It was during this period that he met proof, a respected figure in the Detroit hip-hop community who would become a close friend and mentor.

The influence of Detroit's unique musical heritage on Marshall's developing style was profound. The city's legacy of Motown, rock, and hip-hop provided a rich tapestry of sounds and styles from which he could draw inspiration. This eclectic background would later manifest in his willingness to experiment with different genres and production styles.

Marshall's growing reputation in the local scene led to his first attempts at recording. Working with makeshift equipment in basements and small studios, he produced rough demos that captured his raw talent. These early recordings, while unpolished, showcased his unique voice and lyrical prowess.

The young rapper's involvement in the Detroit scene also exposed him to the harsh realities of the music industry. He witnessed firsthand the struggles of talented artists trying to break through, the pitfalls of bad deals, and the cutthroat nature of the business. These experiences would later inform his approach to his own career and his interactions with the industry.

Marshall's participation in the Detroit rap scene was not without its setbacks. He faced numerous rejections, disappointing performances, and moments of self-doubt. However, each failure only served to fuel his determination. He used these experiences as motivation, channeling his frustrations into his lyrics and performances.

The underground nature of Detroit's rap scene in the 1990s fostered a DIY ethic that would stay with Marshall throughout his career. He learned the importance of self-promotion, networking, and perseverance. These skills would prove invaluable as he navigated the path to stardom.

Marshall's time in the Detroit rap scene also saw the beginning of his experimentation with different personas and voices in his music. He began to develop characters and alter egos in his rhymes, laying the groundwork for what would eventually become Slim Shady.

CHAPTER 2

2.2 Creation of the Slim Shady Persona

The birth of Slim Shady marked a watershed moment in Marshall Mathers' artistic evolution. This alter ego, born from the depths of his psyche and nurtured by his experiences in Detroit's unforgiving rap scene, would become the vehicle through which he would shock, entertain, and ultimately conquer the world of hip-hop.

Slim Shady emerged as a response to Marshall's frustrations with his early career struggles and personal life challenges. This persona allowed him to express his darkest thoughts and most controversial ideas without the constraints of social norms or personal inhibitions. Slim Shady became the uncensored voice of Marshall's id, saying the unsayable and reveling in provocation.

The creation of Slim Shady was not a sudden event, but rather a gradual evolution. Marshall had long experimented with different voices and characters in his rhymes, but Slim Shady represented something more fully formed and potent. This alter ego allowed him to explore themes of violence, drug use, and deviant behavior in a way that was both shocking and darkly humorous.

Slim Shady's lyrical content pushed the boundaries of acceptability in hip-hop. The persona gave voice to Marshall's most outrageous fantasies and deepest anxieties, often blurring the line between reality and fiction. This approach was controversial, but it also set him apart from other rappers, garnering attention and sparking intense debates about artistic expression and social responsibility.

The visual aspect of the Slim Shady persona was carefully crafted to match its audacious lyrical content. Marshall adopted a distinctive look, bleaching his hair platinum blonde and favoring baggy clothes and a mischievous smirk. This image became instantly recognizable, a visual shorthand for the outrageous content of his music.

Slim Shady allowed Marshall to address his personal demons in a unique way. Through this alter ego, he could confront his troubled relationship with his mother, his experiences of poverty and violence, and his struggles with identity. The persona became a therapeutic outlet, allowing him to process his pain and anger through art.

The creation of Slim Shady also represented a savvy marketing move. Marshall recognized that this larger-than-life character could capture attention in a crowded music marketplace. Slim Shady was designed to provoke, to make people uncomfortable, and ultimately, to be unforgettable.

The development of the Slim Shady persona coincided with Marshall's growing technical skills as a rapper. He used this character to showcase his complex rhyme schemes, rapid-fire delivery, and clever wordplay. Slim Shady became the perfect vehicle for demonstrating his lyrical prowess.

The reaction to Slim Shady in the Detroit rap scene was mixed. Some were impressed by the boldness and originality of the persona, while others were put off by its controversial content. However, the character undeniably made an impact, helping Marshall to stand out in a competitive environment.

Slim Shady also allowed Marshall to explore different narrative techniques in his music. He could tell stories from multiple perspectives, create complex characters, and play with the concept of unreliable narration. This approach added depth and complexity to his music, elevating it beyond simple shock value.

The creation of Slim Shady represented a turning point in Marshall's career. It was through this persona that he would catch the attention of Dr. Dre and secure his major label deal. Slim Shady became the key that unlocked the door to stardom.

2.3 The Slim Shady EP and Catching Dr. Dre's Attention

The Slim Shady EP, released in 1997, represented a crucial stepping stone in Marshall Mathers' journey to hip-hop superstardom. This independent release, produced on a shoestring budget, would serve as the catalyst that propelled him from the underground Detroit rap scene to the attention of one of hip-hop's most influential figures, Dr. Dre.

Recorded in collaboration with the Bass Brothers, who would become long-time producers for Eminem, the EP showcased Marshall's unique style and the fully realized Slim Shady persona. Tracks like "Just Don't Give a Fuck" and "Murder, Murder" displayed his technical prowess as a rapper and his willingness to push lyrical boundaries.

The EP's production, while raw and unpolished by major label standards, perfectly complemented Marshall's aggressive delivery and controversial content. The lo-fi sound lent an air of authenticity to the project, aligning with the gritty, uncompromising image of Slim Shady.

Distribution of the Slim Shady EP was a grassroots effort. Marshall and his team hand-sold copies at shows, independent record stores, and out of the trunk of his car. This DIY approach, born of necessity, helped to build a loyal local following and create buzz around the Slim Shady name.

The EP's impact on the Detroit hip-hop scene was significant. It stood out for its originality, dark humor, and technical skill. Word of mouth spread rapidly, with hip-hop heads passing copies among themselves and discussing the shocking new talent that had emerged from their city.

Critical reception of the Slim Shady EP was mixed but largely positive. Local music critics praised Marshall's lyrical ability and unique perspective, while expressing concern over the violent and misogynistic content. This controversy only served to increase interest in the project.

The Slim Shady EP's journey from Detroit to the ears of Dr. Dre is the stuff of hip-hop legend. A copy of the EP made its way to Jimmy Iovine, co-founder of Interscope Records, through Marshall's manager Paul Rosenberg. Impressed by what he heard, Iovine played the EP for Dr. Dre, who was immediately struck by Marshall's raw talent and unique style.

Dr. Dre's interest in Marshall was piqued by several aspects of the Slim Shady EP. The technical skill displayed in Marshall's rapid-fire delivery and complex rhyme schemes was undeniable. Moreover, the boldness of the Slim Shady persona and the controversial content of the lyrics aligned with Dr. Dre's own history of pushing boundaries in hip-hop.

The track that particularly caught Dr. Dre's attention was "Just Don't Give a Fuck." This song encapsulated everything that made Marshall unique - his biting humor, his willingness to tackle taboo subjects, and his masterful control of rhythm and rhyme. It was this track that convinced Dr. Dre that he needed to work with this new talent.

Dr. Dre's decision to sign Marshall to Aftermath Entertainment was a pivotal moment in hip-hop history. It represented a bridging of two generations of rap, with one of the genre's most respected producers throwing his weight behind a controversial new voice.

The collaboration between Marshall and Dr. Dre would prove to be transformative for both artists. For Marshall, it provided access to top-tier production and a major label platform. For Dr. Dre, it offered the opportunity to work with a fresh, innovative talent who could help revitalize his Aftermath label.

The Slim Shady EP served as a blueprint for what would become "The Slim Shady LP," Marshall's major label debut. Many of the themes, stylistic elements, and even specific lyrics from the EP would be refined and expanded upon in this groundbreaking album.

The success of the Slim Shady EP and the subsequent attention from Dr. Dre validated Marshall's artistic choices. It proved that his uncompromising approach to content and his technically sophisticated style could find an audience beyond the Detroit underground.

The EP also demonstrated Marshall's ability to create a cohesive project that maintained a consistent tone and narrative throughout. This skill would serve him well in crafting the concept albums that would become a hallmark of his later career.

The journey of the Slim Shady EP from local release to the catalyst for a major label deal is a testament to the power of grassroots promotion and word-of-mouth in the music industry. It shows how raw talent, combined with relentless hustle, can cut through the noise and reach the right ears.

The EP's role in catching Dr. Dre's attention also highlights the importance of timing in the music industry. Marshall's unique style arrived at a moment when hip-hop was ready for a new voice, and Dr. Dre was in a position to amplify that voice to a global audience.

The Slim Shady EP stands as a crucial document in hip-hop history, capturing the moment when one of the genre's most influential artists was on the cusp of stardom. It provides a raw, unfiltered look at the talent that would soon reshape the landscape of popular music.

CHAPTER 3

Breakthrough with Dr. Dre

3.1 Signing with Aftermath Entertainment

The pivotal moment in Marshall Mathers' career arrived when he signed with Aftermath Entertainment, Dr. Dre's record label. This partnership would catapult the young rapper from Detroit's underground scene to the forefront of global hip-hop, forever changing the landscape of popular music.

Dr. Dre's decision to sign Marshall was not without controversy. The idea of a white rapper from Detroit joining a label known for its West Coast gangsta rap sound raised eyebrows in the industry. However, Dre's intuition about Marshall's potential would prove to be prescient.

The signing process itself was a whirlwind. After hearing the Slim Shady EP, Dre flew Marshall out to Los Angeles for a meeting. The chemistry between the two artists was immediate and electric. They spent hours in the studio, with Marshall freestyling over Dre's beats, showcasing the raw talent that had caught the producer's attention.

Negotiations for the deal were intense. Marshall's team, led by manager Paul Rosenberg, worked tirelessly to ensure that the contract would be fair and beneficial for their client. The final agreement not only brought Marshall onto Aftermath but also established a joint venture with Interscope Records, providing a broader platform for his music.

The news of Marshall's signing sent shockwaves through the hip-hop community. Many were skeptical about a white rapper from the Midwest joining a label synonymous with West Coast hip-hop. Others recognized the potential for a groundbreaking collaboration between two unique talents.

Marshall's arrival at Aftermath coincided with a crucial period for the label. Dr. Dre had faced several setbacks and was looking for a fresh voice to reinvigorate his brand. The young rapper from Detroit, with his provocative lyrics and undeniable skill, seemed like the perfect candidate to breathe new life into Aftermath.

The cultural significance of this signing cannot be overstated. It represented a bridging of regional and racial divides in hip-hop, challenging preconceptions about who could succeed in the genre. Marshall's partnership with Dre would prove to be a turning point in the mainstreaming of hip-hop culture.

Joining Aftermath meant that Marshall now had access to world-class production and industry resources. This leap from the DIY ethos of the Detroit underground to a major label environment presented both

CHAPTER 3

opportunities and challenges. Marshall would need to adapt to new ways of working while maintaining the raw energy that had made him stand out.

The signing also marked a personal milestone for Marshall. After years of struggle and rejection, he had finally achieved his dream of securing a major label deal. This validation of his talent and hard work provided a much-needed boost to his confidence and motivation.

However, the move to Aftermath also brought new pressures. Marshall was now under intense scrutiny, with high expectations from both the label and the hip-hop community. He would need to prove that he could translate his underground success to the mainstream without compromising his artistic vision.

The partnership between Marshall and Dr. Dre extended beyond just a typical artist-label relationship. Dre took on a mentorship role, guiding the young rapper through the intricacies of the music industry and helping him refine his sound. This collaborative approach would prove crucial in shaping Marshall's debut album for Aftermath.

Signing with Aftermath also meant relocating to Los Angeles, a significant change for the Detroit native. This geographical shift would influence Marshall's music, exposing him to new sounds and experiences that would find their way into his lyrics.

The deal with Aftermath set the stage for what would become one of the most successful and influential careers in hip-hop history. It provided Marshall with the platform he needed to bring his unique voice and perspective to a global audience, forever changing the face of popular music.

3.2 Recording The Slim Shady LP

The recording of "The Slim Shady LP" marked a transformative period in Marshall Mathers' career, bridging his underground roots with the polished production of a major label release. This process would result in an album that not only launched Eminem into superstardom but also reshaped the landscape of hip-hop.

Recording sessions for the album began in earnest following Marshall's signing to Aftermath Entertainment. Dr. Dre's state-of-the-art studio in Los Angeles provided a stark contrast to the makeshift setups Marshall had used in Detroit. This new environment, coupled with access to top-tier equipment and production talent, opened up new sonic possibilities for the young rapper.

Dr. Dre's hands-on approach to the album's production was crucial in shaping its sound. His beats provided a perfect backdrop for Marshall's rapid-fire delivery and complex rhyme schemes. The combination of Dre's West Coast funk-influenced production with Marshall's Midwest rap style created a unique sonic palette that set the album apart from contemporary hip-hop releases.

The writing process for "The Slim Shady LP" was intense and deeply personal. Marshall drew heavily from his experiences in Detroit, his struggles with poverty and family issues, and the persona of Slim Shady he had developed. Many of the lyrics were shocking and controversial, pushing the boundaries of what was considered acceptable in mainstream music.

Collaborations played a key role in the album's creation. While Dr. Dre was the primary producer, Marshall also worked with the Bass

CHAPTER 3

Brothers, who had produced his independent EP. This blend of familiar collaborators and new influences helped to create a sound that was both fresh and true to Marshall's roots.

The recording sessions were not without their challenges. Marshall, used to the DIY approach of the Detroit scene, initially struggled to adapt to the more structured environment of a major label studio. However, he quickly learned to harness these new resources to enhance his art rather than constrain it.

Tensions occasionally arose during the recording process, particularly regarding the album's content. Some executives expressed concern about the graphic nature of certain lyrics and the potential backlash they might provoke. However, both Marshall and Dr. Dre stood firm in their artistic vision, refusing to water down the album's content.

The creation of "My Name Is," the album's lead single, was a pivotal moment in the recording process. The track, with its catchy hook and irreverent lyrics, perfectly encapsulated the Slim Shady persona. Its potential as a breakthrough hit was immediately apparent to everyone involved in the project.

Throughout the recording, Marshall maintained a grueling work schedule, often spending 16-hour days in the studio. This dedication to his craft is evident in the intricate wordplay and complex narratives that characterize the album. Every line was meticulously crafted and delivered with precision.

The album's skits, a hallmark of Eminem's style, were largely improvised during the recording sessions. These interludes provided comic relief and helped to create a cohesive narrative throughout the album, enhancing the world-building aspect of the Slim Shady persona.

Mixing and mastering the album presented its own set of challenges. Balancing Marshall's vocal delivery with Dre's bass-heavy beats required careful attention to detail. The final mix needed to preserve the raw energy of Marshall's performance while meeting the sound quality standards of a major label release.

As the recording process neared its end, there was a palpable sense of excitement among those involved. It was clear that they had created something special, an album that would not only launch Marshall's career but potentially change the course of hip-hop.

The final track listing was carefully considered, with songs arranged to create a narrative flow that would take listeners on a journey through the world of Slim Shady. This attention to sequencing would become a hallmark of Eminem's albums throughout his career.

With the recording complete, "The Slim Shady LP" was ready to be unleashed on the world. The album represented the culmination of Marshall's journey from the Detroit underground to the brink of global stardom, a testament to his raw talent and the transformative power of his partnership with Dr. Dre.

3.3 Impact of "My Name Is" and Mainstream Success

The release of "My Name Is" as the lead single from "The Slim Shady LP" marked a seismic shift in the hip-hop landscape. This track, with its infectious beat and audacious lyrics, would serve as the world's introduction to Eminem, catapulting him from underground obscurity

CHAPTER 3

to mainstream notoriety virtually overnight.

The song's impact was immediate and far-reaching. Its accompanying music video, featuring Eminem in various outrageous scenarios, quickly became a staple on MTV. The visual representation of the Slim Shady persona, with its bleached blonde hair and mischievous smirk, became instantly iconic, burning itself into the cultural consciousness.

Radio stations across the country, initially hesitant to play such controversial content, found themselves inundated with requests for the track. "My Name Is" broke through genre barriers, finding airplay not just on hip-hop stations but also on pop and rock formats. This crossover appeal would become a hallmark of Eminem's career.

The lyrical content of "My Name Is" sparked intense debate in the media and among listeners. Its irreverent humor, pop culture references, and willingness to tackle taboo subjects set it apart from other rap hits of the time. Critics and fans alike pored over every line, analyzing the clever wordplay and controversial statements. This scrutiny only served to increase the song's cultural impact.

The success of "My Name Is" paved the way for the broader acceptance of "The Slim Shady LP." The album debuted at number two on the Billboard 200 chart, an unprecedented achievement for a new artist in the hip-hop genre. It would go on to be certified quadruple platinum, solidifying Eminem's place in the mainstream music landscape.

Eminem's rise to fame was not without controversy. Parent groups and conservative organizations decried the violent and sexually explicit content of his lyrics. However, this backlash only seemed to fuel his popularity, particularly among younger listeners who were drawn to his rebellious image.

The mainstream success of "My Name Is" and "The Slim Shady LP" had a profound impact on the hip-hop industry. It demonstrated that a white rapper could achieve widespread commercial success without compromising his artistic integrity or connection to the genre's roots. This opened doors for a new generation of diverse artists in hip-hop.

Eminem's breakthrough also challenged prevailing notions about what constituted "mainstream" music. His unfiltered approach to lyrical content pushed the boundaries of what was considered acceptable in pop culture, influencing not just music but also comedy, film, and television.

The financial success of "The Slim Shady LP" had far-reaching implications for Aftermath Entertainment and Interscope Records. It validated Dr. Dre's instincts about Eminem's potential and provided a much-needed hit for the label. This success would allow Dre to take more risks with future signings, further shaping the direction of hip-hop.

Eminem's rapid ascent to stardom brought with it a new set of challenges. The young rapper from Detroit now found himself thrust into the global spotlight, dealing with intense media scrutiny and the pressures of fame. His struggles with this newfound celebrity would become a recurring theme in his future work.

The success of "My Name Is" and "The Slim Shady LP" also had a significant impact on Eminem's personal life. His tumultuous relationship with his mother, a frequent target in his lyrics, became a matter of public discourse. His ex-wife Kim and daughter Hailie were also thrust into the spotlight, adding new layers of complexity to his already complicated personal life.

Eminem's breakthrough sparked debates about authenticity in hip-hop. Some purists questioned whether a white artist from the Midwest could truly represent the genre. However, Eminem's undeniable skill and his respect for hip-hop culture gradually won over many of his critics within the industry.

The massive success of "My Name Is" set a high bar for Eminem's future releases. Each subsequent single and album would be measured against the impact of his breakthrough hit. This pressure to continually innovate and shock would drive Eminem's creative process for years to come.

Eminem's mainstream success also had a significant impact on Detroit's hip-hop scene. His rise to fame put a spotlight on the city's vibrant underground rap culture, opening doors for other Detroit artists and producers. The success of "The Slim Shady LP" helped to establish Detroit as a major player in the hip-hop world.

The critical acclaim that accompanied Eminem's commercial success further cemented his position in the music industry. "The Slim Shady LP" received widespread praise for its technical proficiency, dark humor, and unflinching honesty. This critical recognition, culminating in a Grammy Award for Best Rap Album, validated Eminem as a serious artist beyond just a controversial figure.

Eminem's breakthrough also represented a shift in the power dynamics of the music industry. His success demonstrated the potential of viral, word-of-mouth marketing in the emerging digital age. The controversy surrounding his lyrics, spread through online forums and early social media, proved to be a powerful promotional tool.

The impact of "My Name Is" and "The Slim Shady LP" extended beyond the realm of music into popular culture at large. Eminem's unique style, both musically and visually, was widely imitated and parodied. His influence could be seen in fashion, slang, and even in the way people engaged with and discussed controversial topics.

In the years following the release of "My Name Is" and "The Slim Shady LP," Eminem's influence on the music industry only continued to grow. He had not just achieved mainstream success; he had fundamentally altered the landscape of popular music, challenging preconceptions about race, content, and artistry in hip-hop. His breakthrough marked the beginning of a career that would continue to push boundaries and redefine the possibilities of rap music for years to come.

4

CHAPTER 4

The Marshall Mathers LP: Cementing Legendary Status

4.1 Creation and Themes of the Album

The creation of "The Marshall Mathers LP" marked a pivotal moment in Eminem's career, solidifying his place as a hip-hop icon and cultural phenomenon. Following the massive success of "The Slim Shady LP," Eminem faced immense pressure to deliver a worthy follow-up. This pressure, combined with his newfound fame and personal struggles, provided fertile ground for the creation of what many consider his magnum opus.

Recording for the album began in late 1999, with Eminem working tirelessly in the studio to craft a body of work that would surpass his previous efforts. The production team, led by Dr. Dre and including the Bass Brothers, created a sonic palette that perfectly complemented

Eminem's intense, introspective lyrics. The beats were darker and more complex than those on "The Slim Shady LP," reflecting the heavier themes explored in the album.

Lyrically, "The Marshall Mathers LP" delved deep into Eminem's psyche, exploring themes of fame, family, and identity with unflinching honesty. The rapper's relationship with his mother, a recurring subject in his work, was examined in even greater detail, most notably in the track "Kill You." This song, with its violent imagery and dark humor, exemplified Eminem's ability to shock while also providing commentary on his troubled upbringing.

The album's exploration of fame and its consequences was particularly poignant. Tracks like "The Way I Am" and "Marshall Mathers" saw Eminem grappling with his sudden rise to stardom and the pressures that came with it. He railed against the media, his critics, and even his fans, painting a vivid picture of the isolation and paranoia that accompanied his newfound celebrity status.

Eminem's alter ego, Slim Shady, featured prominently on the album, allowing the rapper to explore his darkest impulses and most controversial ideas. The interplay between Eminem's various personas - Marshall Mathers, Slim Shady, and Eminem - created a complex narrative structure that added depth and nuance to the album's themes.

The creation of "Stan," one of the album's standout tracks, showcased Eminem's growth as a storyteller. This chilling tale of an obsessed fan, told through a series of increasingly desperate letters, demonstrated Eminem's ability to craft compelling narratives and create fully realized characters within the confines of a rap song.

CHAPTER 4

Thematically, the album also tackled broader social issues. "The Real Slim Shady" took aim at pop culture and the music industry, while "Criminal" addressed accusations of homophobia and misogyny that had been leveled against Eminem. These tracks demonstrated the rapper's willingness to engage with his critics head-on, using his music as a platform for both self-defense and social commentary.

The recording process for "The Marshall Mathers LP" was intense and often emotionally draining. Eminem poured his fears, anxieties, and anger into every track, resulting in a raw, unfiltered album that felt like a direct window into the rapper's psyche. This emotional honesty resonated strongly with listeners, contributing to the album's massive impact.

Musically, the album saw Eminem continuing to push the boundaries of his technical skills. His flow became even more complex, with intricate rhyme schemes and rapid-fire delivery that showcased his growing mastery of the craft. The production, while still rooted in Dr. Dre's signature sound, incorporated a wider range of musical influences, from rock to classical.

The creation of "The Marshall Mathers LP" also involved a number of high-profile collaborations. Dido's haunting vocals on "Stan" provided a perfect counterpoint to Eminem's intense delivery, while appearances by Dr. Dre, Snoop Dogg, and Xzibit added variety to the album's sound. These collaborations helped to broaden Eminem's appeal while still maintaining his unique artistic vision.

Throughout the creation of the album, Eminem remained committed to his artistic integrity, refusing to compromise his vision despite pressure from the label and concerns about potential controversy. This unwavering commitment to his art would prove crucial in establishing "The Marshall Mathers LP" as a landmark album in hip-hop history.

4.2 Controversy and Critical Acclaim

The release of "The Marshall Mathers LP" in May 2000 ignited a firestorm of controversy that would cement Eminem's status as one of the most polarizing figures in popular music. The album's graphic content, violent imagery, and provocative lyrics sparked intense debate across society, from living rooms to legislative chambers.

Critics and advocacy groups were quick to condemn the album's content. The Parents Music Resource Center (PMRC) and other conservative organizations called for boycotts, arguing that Eminem's lyrics promoted violence, misogyny, and homophobia. These accusations led to heated discussions about censorship, artistic freedom, and the responsibility of artists in society.

The track "Kim," a visceral depiction of domestic violence, became a particular flashpoint for controversy. Its graphic portrayal of a murder-suicide scenario involving Eminem and his wife drew sharp criticism from women's rights organizations. The rapper's use of homophobic slurs throughout the album also attracted condemnation from LGBTQ+ advocacy groups.

Politicians seized upon the controversy, with several U.S. Senators calling for federal regulation of the music industry. Eminem found himself at the center of a national debate about free speech and the limits of artistic expression. This political attention only served to increase the album's notoriety and fuel public interest.

CHAPTER 4

Media coverage of "The Marshall Mathers LP" was extensive and often sensationalized. News programs and talk shows debated the merits and dangers of Eminem's music, often featuring heated exchanges between supporters and detractors. This constant media attention kept the album in the public eye for months after its release.

Amidst the controversy, many critics praised the album for its artistic merits. Music journalists lauded Eminem's technical skill, his complex rhyme schemes, and his ability to craft compelling narratives. The album's production, primarily handled by Dr. Dre and the Bass Brothers, also received widespread acclaim for its innovative sound.

Critics noted the album's raw emotional honesty, praising Eminem's willingness to expose his vulnerabilities and confront his demons in his lyrics. Many viewed the violent and controversial content as a reflection of societal ills rather than a glorification of negative behavior. This interpretation helped to legitimize the album as a serious work of art rather than mere sensationalism.

The track "Stan" received particular critical acclaim. Its innovative storytelling format and exploration of fan culture were hailed as groundbreaking. Many critics cited this song as evidence of Eminem's growth as an artist, demonstrating his ability to move beyond shock tactics to create nuanced, thought-provoking music.

Eminem's technical prowess as a rapper was universally recognized, even by his harshest critics. His complex rhyme schemes, clever wordplay, and ability to change flow mid-verse were praised as pushing the boundaries of what was possible in hip-hop. This technical skill helped to establish Eminem as a respected figure within the hip-hop community.

The album's exploration of fame and its consequences resonated with many critics. Eminem's unflinching examination of his own sudden rise to stardom and its impact on his psyche was seen as a refreshingly honest take on celebrity culture. This theme helped to contextualize the album's more controversial elements as part of a larger artistic statement.

Debates about the album's content often centered around the distinction between Eminem's various personas. Critics argued over whether the violent and misogynistic lyrics should be attributed to Eminem himself or to his Slim Shady alter ego. This discussion highlighted the complex nature of artistic identity and the role of persona in hip-hop.

The controversy surrounding "The Marshall Mathers LP" extended to the international stage. Several countries considered banning Eminem from performing, citing concerns about the content of his lyrics. These international incidents further fueled the album's notoriety and contributed to its global impact.

Music industry insiders, while sometimes critical of the album's content, recognized its significance. Many praised Eminem and his team for pushing the boundaries of what was possible in mainstream music. The album was seen as a watershed moment in hip-hop's evolution from a niche genre to a dominant force in popular culture.

The critical discourse surrounding "The Marshall Mathers LP" often touched on larger issues of race in America. Eminem's position as a white artist in a predominantly black genre led to discussions about cultural appropriation and authenticity in hip-hop. These debates helped to highlight the complex racial dynamics at play in popular music.

CHAPTER 4

Academic interest in the album further legitimized its artistic value. Scholars in fields ranging from musicology to sociology began analyzing Eminem's work, examining its cultural significance and artistic merits. This academic attention helped to elevate the album's status beyond mere popular entertainment to a subject worthy of serious study.

4.3 Commercial Success and Grammy Awards

The commercial success of "The Marshall Mathers LP" was nothing short of phenomenal, shattering records and setting new benchmarks for the music industry. Upon its release in May 2000, the album debuted at number one on the Billboard 200 chart, selling a staggering 1.76 million copies in its first week. This feat made it the fastest-selling studio album by any solo artist in American music history at that time.

The album's sales momentum continued unabated in the weeks and months following its release. By the end of 2000, "The Marshall Mathers LP" had sold over 7.9 million copies in the United States alone, making it the second best-selling album of the year. Its popularity extended far beyond American shores, with the album topping charts in numerous countries around the world.

Singles from the album dominated radio airplay and music video rotation. "The Real Slim Shady," the lead single, became an instant hit, reaching number four on the Billboard Hot 100 and earning heavy rotation on MTV. The controversial nature of the song and its accompanying video only served to increase its popularity, making it a cultural touchstone of the early 2000s.

"Stan," featuring a sample from Dido's "Thank You," became another massive hit from the album. Its innovative narrative structure and haunting melody captivated audiences, and the term "stan" entered the popular lexicon as a term for an overzealous fan. The song's music video, directed by Dr. Dre and Philip Atwell, was praised for its cinematic quality and further cemented the track's iconic status.

The album's commercial success extended to the realm of music streaming as the technology became more prevalent. Years after its initial release, "The Marshall Mathers LP" continued to rack up millions of streams across various platforms, introducing Eminem's magnum opus to new generations of listeners.

The Recording Industry Association of America (RIAA) certified "The Marshall Mathers LP" Diamond in March 2011, signifying sales of over 10 million copies in the United States. This achievement placed Eminem in an elite group of artists who have achieved multiple Diamond-certified albums, further solidifying his status as one of the best-selling music artists of all time.

The album's commercial triumph was not limited to sales figures. It also garnered critical acclaim and industry recognition, culminating in multiple Grammy Award nominations. At the 43rd Annual Grammy Awards in 2001, "The Marshall Mathers LP" was nominated for Album of the Year, making Eminem the first white rapper to receive this honor.

While the album didn't win Album of the Year, it did secure the Grammy for Best Rap Album, marking Eminem's second consecutive win in this category. This victory underscored the album's impact within the hip-hop community and its role in bringing rap music further into the mainstream.

CHAPTER 4

"The Real Slim Shady" won the Grammy for Best Rap Solo Performance, adding to Eminem's growing collection of accolades. The song's win was particularly significant given its controversial content, demonstrating the Recording Academy's recognition of Eminem's artistic merit despite (or perhaps because of) his provocative approach.

Eminem's performance of "Stan" at the Grammy Awards ceremony, featuring Elton John on piano and vocals, became one of the most memorable moments in the show's history. This unexpected collaboration, which came amidst accusations of homophobia against Eminem, helped to soften his image and showcased his ability to transcend genre boundaries.

The commercial success and critical acclaim of "The Marshall Mathers LP" had far-reaching effects on Eminem's career and the music industry as a whole. It established him as a global superstar, capable of achieving pop culture dominance while maintaining his hip-hop credibility. The album's success also paved the way for hip-hop to become the dominant force in popular music that it is today.

The financial windfall from the album's success allowed Eminem to expand his business ventures. He launched Shady Records, his own record label imprint under Interscope, which would go on to sign and develop numerous successful artists. This move into the business side of the industry further cemented Eminem's influence on hip-hop culture.

The album's commercial triumph also had a significant impact on Eminem's personal life. The massive influx of wealth and fame brought new challenges, many of which would be explored in his subsequent works. The tension between his public persona and private life, a key theme in "The Marshall Mathers LP," would only intensify in the wake of the album's success.

The Grammy recognition for "The Marshall Mathers LP" marked a turning point in the Recording Academy's relationship with hip-hop. While rap had been acknowledged by the Grammys before, Eminem's nominations and wins in major categories helped to legitimize the genre in the eyes of the music industry establishment.

The enduring commercial success of "The Marshall Mathers LP" has cemented its place in the pantheon of classic albums. Its continued strong sales and streaming numbers years after its release speak to its timeless appeal and its status as a defining work of its era. The album remains a benchmark against which both Eminem's later works and those of other rap artists are measured.

In the years following its release, "The Marshall Mathers LP" has been featured prominently in various "greatest albums" lists compiled by music publications and critics. Its inclusion in these lists, often ranking highly among albums from all genres, further underscores its lasting impact and critical standing.

The commercial and critical success of "The Marshall Mathers LP" ultimately transformed Eminem from a controversial rapper into a bona fide pop culture icon. It solidified his status as one of the most significant artists of his generation, and its influence continues to be felt in the worlds of music, pop culture, and beyond.

CHAPTER 5

The Eminem Show and Growing Fame

5.1 Development of Eminem's Sound and Style

"The Eminem Show" marked a significant evolution in Eminem's artistry, showcasing a more mature and introspective approach to his music. Released in 2002, the album represented a departure from the shock tactics and extreme controversy that characterized his earlier work, instead focusing on deeper personal reflections and social commentary.

Eminem's lyrical content on "The Eminem Show" delved into more complex territory. He explored themes of fatherhood, political issues, and his place in the hip-hop landscape with a newfound depth and nuance. Tracks like "Cleanin' Out My Closet" and "Sing for the Moment" demonstrated his ability to craft emotionally resonant narratives that went beyond the shock value of his previous albums.

The production on "The Eminem Show" also saw a significant shift. Eminem took a more hands-on approach to the album's sound, producing the majority of the tracks himself. This resulted in a more cohesive sonic palette that perfectly complemented his lyrical themes. The beats were often guitar-driven, incorporating elements of rock music into his hip-hop foundation.

Eminem's flow and delivery on this album showcased his continued technical growth as a rapper. His rhyme schemes became even more complex, with internal rhymes and assonance woven intricately throughout his verses. His ability to switch between rapid-fire delivery and more measured, emotional performances demonstrated his versatility as an artist.

The album's content reflected Eminem's growing awareness of his influence and responsibility as a public figure. He addressed criticisms of his work head-on, using tracks like "White America" to examine the racial dynamics of his success in the hip-hop world. This self-awareness added a new dimension to his artistry, making his work more thought-provoking and less reliant on shock value.

Eminem's use of alter egos evolved on "The Eminem Show." While Slim Shady still made appearances, the album saw more of Marshall Mathers, the man behind the persona, coming to the forefront. This shift allowed for a more authentic and personal expression of his experiences and emotions.

The incorporation of live instrumentation on many tracks gave "The Eminem Show" a fuller, more organic sound compared to his previous albums. This musical evolution reflected Eminem's growing interest in expanding his sonic palette beyond traditional hip-hop production.

CHAPTER 5

Eminem's storytelling abilities reached new heights on this album. Tracks like "Say Goodbye Hollywood" and "Hailie's Song" painted vivid pictures of his personal life and struggles with fame, showcasing his talent for narrative songwriting. These songs demonstrated his ability to connect with listeners on a deeply emotional level.

The album's skits and interludes were more integrated into the overall narrative, serving to enhance the themes explored in the songs rather than merely providing comic relief. This approach created a more cohesive listening experience, reinforcing the album's conceptual nature.

Eminem's vocal performances on "The Eminem Show" displayed a wider emotional range than on previous albums. From the vulnerability displayed in "Hailie's Song" to the righteous anger of "Square Dance," he proved capable of conveying a broad spectrum of feelings through his music.

The lyrical content of "The Eminem Show" revealed a more politically engaged Eminem. Tracks like "Mosh" and "Square Dance" saw him tackling issues like the War on Terror and American politics, demonstrating his growing willingness to use his platform for social commentary.

Eminem's collaborations on this album were more selective and meaningful. The featured artists, including Dr. Dre and Nate Dogg, were used sparingly but effectively, enhancing the songs without overshadowing Eminem's central narrative.

The album's cover art and overall aesthetic reflected the more serious tone of the music. The image of Eminem taking a bow on stage symbolized his acknowledgment of his role as an entertainer while also hinting at the personal nature of the album's content.

Eminem's growth as a producer was evident throughout "The Eminem Show." His beats became more layered and complex, incorporating a wide range of samples and original compositions. This development allowed him greater control over his artistic vision, resulting in a more cohesive and personal album.

The maturation of Eminem's sound and style on "The Eminem Show" set the stage for his continued evolution as an artist. It demonstrated his ability to grow beyond the shock rapper label and establish himself as a multifaceted musician capable of creating thoughtful, introspective work.

5.2 Hit Singles and Album Reception

"The Eminem Show" produced several hit singles that dominated airwaves and music video channels, further solidifying Eminem's position as a pop culture icon. The lead single, "Without Me," became an instant classic, showcasing Eminem's signature wit and wordplay over a catchy, upbeat production. The song's music video, featuring Eminem in various comedic scenarios, received heavy rotation on MTV and won the Video of the Year award at the 2002 MTV Video Music Awards.

"Cleanin' Out My Closet," the album's second single, marked a departure from Eminem's typically humorous approach. This intensely personal track, which delved into his troubled relationship with his mother, resonated deeply with listeners and critics alike. Its raw emotion and unflinching honesty helped to humanize Eminem in the public eye,

CHAPTER 5

moving beyond his controversial persona to reveal the man behind the music.

The third single, "Sing for the Moment," which sampled Aerosmith's "Dream On," became an anthem for Eminem's impact on his young fans. The song addressed criticisms of his influence on youth culture while also acknowledging the power of music to inspire and comfort. Its rock-influenced sound showcased Eminem's ability to blend genres effectively.

"Superman," featuring backing vocals from Dina Rae, became another hit from the album. Its exploration of dysfunctional relationships and trust issues provided yet another dimension to Eminem's artistic repertoire. The song's popularity demonstrated Eminem's ability to tackle a wide range of subjects while maintaining his commercial appeal.

Critical reception of "The Eminem Show" was overwhelmingly positive. Many reviewers praised the album for its musical and lyrical maturity, noting Eminem's growth as both a rapper and a producer. The album's more introspective and politically charged content was particularly well-received, with critics appreciating Eminem's willingness to tackle serious issues.

The album's exploration of fame and its consequences resonated strongly with critics and fans alike. Many saw it as a thoughtful examination of Eminem's place in the music industry and popular culture at large. The honesty with which he addressed his struggles with celebrity was widely praised.

Eminem's technical skills as a rapper were universally lauded. Critics noted his increasingly complex rhyme schemes, clever wordplay, and ability to convey a wide range of emotions through his delivery. Many considered "The Eminem Show" to be his most accomplished work to date in terms of pure rap technique.

The album's production, largely handled by Eminem himself, also received significant praise. Critics appreciated the fuller, more organic sound, noting how well it complemented Eminem's lyrics. The incorporation of rock elements was seen as a successful evolution of his sound.

"The Eminem Show" debuted at number one on the Billboard 200 chart, selling over 1.3 million copies in its first full week of release. It remained at the top of the charts for five consecutive weeks and was certified Diamond by the RIAA, signifying sales of over 10 million copies in the United States alone.

The album's commercial success extended globally, topping charts in numerous countries and solidifying Eminem's status as an international superstar. Its worldwide sales further established him as one of the best-selling music artists of all time.

At the 45th Annual Grammy Awards, "The Eminem Show" won the award for Best Rap Album, marking Eminem's third consecutive win in this category. The album was also nominated for Album of the Year, further cementing its critical acclaim.

The singles from "The Eminem Show" performed exceptionally well on the charts. "Without Me" reached number two on the Billboard Hot 100, while "Cleanin' Out My Closet" and "Sing for the Moment" both reached the top ten. These chart performances demonstrated the album's broad appeal and Eminem's ability to create hit singles across various styles.

The music videos for the album's singles were widely praised for their creativity and production value. The video for "Without Me," in particular, became iconic, with its numerous pop culture references and Eminem's comedic performances. These videos helped to further expand Eminem's visual aesthetic and cement his place in popular culture.

The success of "The Eminem Show" had a significant impact on the music industry as a whole. It helped to further mainstream hip-hop, bringing the genre to an even wider audience. The album's blend of personal narratives, social commentary, and pop culture references set a new standard for what could be achieved in mainstream rap music.

In the years following its release, "The Eminem Show" has been consistently ranked as one of the greatest hip-hop albums of all time. Its influence can be heard in the work of numerous artists who followed, both in terms of its lyrical content and its sonic palette. The album's success paved the way for more introspective and politically engaged rap music to find mainstream success.

The album's reception also marked a shift in how Eminem was perceived by the media and the public. While still controversial, he was increasingly viewed as a serious artist rather than merely a provocateur. This changing perception allowed for more nuanced discussions of his work and its impact on popular culture.

5.3 Balancing Fame and Personal Life

The monumental success of "The Eminem Show" catapulted Eminem to unprecedented levels of fame, bringing with it a host of new challenges in his personal life. The rapper found himself struggling to maintain a sense of normalcy amidst the constant scrutiny and demands of his public persona.

Eminem's relationship with his daughter, Hailie, became a central concern during this period. He was determined to be a present and loving father, despite the pressures of his career. Tracks like "Hailie's Song" on "The Eminem Show" reflected this dedication, offering a glimpse into his softer side and his priorities beyond music.

The intense media attention surrounding Eminem began to take its toll. Paparazzi constantly hounded him, making it difficult to engage in everyday activities without being photographed or harassed. This invasion of privacy led to increasing feelings of paranoia and isolation, themes that would be explored in his subsequent work.

Eminem's tumultuous relationship with his ex-wife, Kim, continued to be a source of personal strife. Their on-again, off-again dynamic played out in the public eye, adding another layer of complexity to his already complicated personal life. The rapper had to navigate co-parenting amid intense public scrutiny and his own conflicted feelings.

Substance abuse issues began to surface more prominently during this period. The pressures of fame, coupled with the physical demands of touring and recording, led Eminem to increasingly rely on prescription medications. This dependency would eventually evolve into a full-blown addiction, impacting both his personal life and his career.

CHAPTER 5

Eminem's rise to superstardom also affected his relationships within the hip-hop community. He found himself navigating a complex web of alliances and rivalries, all while trying to maintain his authenticity as an artist. Balancing his roots in the Detroit rap scene with his new status as a global icon proved challenging.

The rapper's newfound wealth brought its own set of complications. While it provided financial security for himself and his family, it also attracted hangers-on and led to trust issues. Eminem became increasingly guarded, unsure of people's true motives in befriending or working with him.

Eminem's controversial lyrics and public persona continued to generate backlash, leading to protests and calls for boycotts. Balancing his artistic expression with the real-world consequences of his words became an ongoing struggle. He had to consider the impact of his music not just on his career, but on his personal life and the lives of those close to him.

The demands of Eminem's career often conflicted with his desire for privacy and normalcy. Endless promotional obligations, tours, and public appearances left little time for personal relationships or self-care. This constant grind contributed to feelings of burnout and dissatisfaction, despite his professional success.

Eminem's relationship with his mother, Debbie, remained strained during this period. While he had addressed their troubled history in his music, the public nature of their conflict added another layer of stress to his personal life. Attempts at reconciliation were complicated by the public's intense interest in their relationship.

The rapper's friendship with proof, his longtime collaborator and member of D12, provided a grounding influence during this turbulent time. Proof served as a link to Eminem's pre-fame life, offering a sense of normalcy and authenticity amidst the chaos of stardom.

Eminem's efforts to maintain his connection to Detroit became increasingly challenging as his fame grew. While he remained committed to his hometown, the realities of his celebrity status made it difficult to move freely or maintain the same level of involvement in the local scene.

The pressure to continually produce hit records and maintain his position at the top of the music industry took a toll on Eminem's mental health. He struggled with anxiety and depression, often feeling trapped by the expectations placed upon him by fans, critics, and his own perfectionist tendencies.

Eminem's role as a mentor and label head for Shady Records added another layer of responsibility to his already full plate. Balancing his own career with the development of new artists required significant time and energy, often at the expense of his personal life.

The rapper's attempts to maintain a semblance of a normal family life were constantly challenged by his fame. Simple activities like attending his daughter's school events or family outings became logistical nightmares, requiring careful planning and security measures.

Throughout this period, Eminem's music served as both an outlet for his personal struggles and a source of additional pressure. Each new release was scrutinized for insights into his private life, making it difficult for him to separate his art from his reality.

CHAPTER 6

Encore and Hiatus

6.1 Release of Encore in 2004

Eminem's fifth studio album, "Encore," hit the shelves on November 12, 2004, amid a flurry of anticipation and speculation. The album arrived at a pivotal moment in the rapper's career, following the massive success of "The Eminem Show" and his starring role in the semi-autobiographical film "8 Mile."

The creation of "Encore" took place during a tumultuous period in Eminem's life. His ongoing struggles with prescription drug addiction, coupled with the pressures of maintaining his position at the top of the music industry, significantly influenced the album's content and tone. These personal battles seeped into the lyrics, resulting in a more erratic and unpredictable collection of songs compared to his previous works.

"Encore" saw Eminem experimenting with new sounds and styles. The production, largely handled by Dr. Dre and Eminem himself, incorporated a wider range of musical elements, including more pronounced use of live instrumentation. This sonic evolution represented Eminem's attempt to push his artistic boundaries and avoid stagnation.

The album's lead single, "Just Lose It," was released on September 28, 2004, and immediately stirred controversy. The song and its accompanying music video, which parodied Michael Jackson among others, drew criticism from various quarters. This controversy set the tone for the album's reception and highlighted Eminem's continued ability to provoke and polarize.

"Encore" featured a mix of serious, introspective tracks and more comedic, outlandish songs. Tracks like "Mosh" showcased Eminem's political engagement, with fierce criticism of the Bush administration and the Iraq War. In contrast, songs like "Ass Like That" leaned heavily into crude humor and shock value, reflecting the conflicted nature of Eminem's artistic direction at the time.

The album's release was marked by an elaborate marketing campaign. Eminem's team employed innovative strategies to generate buzz, including the use of guerrilla marketing tactics and viral internet campaigns. These efforts helped to ensure that "Encore" would debut with massive sales figures.

Eminem's lyrical content on "Encore" continued to mine his personal life for material. Songs like "Puke" and "Love You More" delved into his tumultuous relationship with his ex-wife Kim, while "Mockingbird" offered a heartfelt tribute to his daughter Hailie. These personal narratives provided a counterpoint to the album's more outrageous

CHAPTER 6

moments.

The release of "Encore" was accompanied by a series of high-profile television appearances and interviews. Eminem used these platforms to promote the album and address the various controversies surrounding his work. His public persona during this period oscillated between his trademark irreverence and a newfound weariness with the demands of fame.

Collaborations on "Encore" were relatively sparse compared to Eminem's previous albums. However, the inclusion of 50 Cent and Nate Dogg on "Never Enough" and Dr. Dre and 50 Cent on "Encore/Curtains Down" provided some of the album's standout moments. These collaborations highlighted Eminem's continued connections within the hip-hop community.

The physical release of "Encore" included elaborate packaging and bonus content, reflecting the music industry's efforts to combat piracy and declining CD sales. A limited edition version of the album included a bonus disc with additional tracks, providing added value for dedicated fans.

"Encore" debuted at number one on the Billboard 200 chart, selling over 710,000 copies in its first three days of release. This impressive opening week set the stage for the album's commercial success, though it fell short of the record-breaking numbers achieved by "The Eminem Show."

The album's cover art, featuring Eminem taking a bow in front of a red curtain, played on the theatrical themes suggested by the title. This imagery hinted at the performative aspects of Eminem's career and the blurred lines between his public persona and private self.

The release of "Encore" coincided with a period of increased scrutiny of the music industry's marketing tactics. The album's parental advisory sticker and controversial content reignited debates about censorship and artistic freedom in popular music.

Eminem's promotional efforts for "Encore" included a series of elaborate music videos. The video for "Like Toy Soldiers," which addressed Eminem's various hip-hop feuds, was particularly notable for its cinematic quality and serious tone, contrasting with the more comedic videos for other singles.

The timing of "Encore's" release, coming just after the 2004 U.S. presidential election, gave added weight to its political content. Songs like "Mosh" resonated with listeners frustrated by the election results and the ongoing war in Iraq, cementing Eminem's status as a voice for disaffected youth.

6.2 Mixed Critical Reception

The critical response to "Encore" was notably divided, marking a departure from the near-universal acclaim that had greeted Eminem's previous albums. Critics grappled with the album's tonal inconsistencies and Eminem's evolving artistic direction, resulting in a wide range of opinions.

Many reviewers praised Eminem's technical skills as a rapper, noting that his complex rhyme schemes and clever wordplay remained impressive. His ability to shift between different flows and personas within a

CHAPTER 6

single track continued to set him apart from his peers in the hip-hop world.

The political content on "Encore," particularly the track "Mosh," received significant attention from critics. Many applauded Eminem's willingness to engage with current events and use his platform to express dissent. This aspect of the album was seen as a mature evolution of his artistry.

However, the album's more comedic tracks drew criticism from many quarters. Songs like "Just Lose It" and "Ass Like That" were derided by some critics as juvenile and a step backward for an artist who had shown significant growth on "The Eminem Show." These tracks were seen by some as Eminem retreating into shock tactics rather than pushing his art forward.

The production on "Encore" received mixed reviews. While some critics appreciated the expanded sonic palette and increased use of live instrumentation, others felt that the beats lacked the punch and memorability of Eminem's earlier work. The diversity of sounds on the album was alternately praised for its ambition and criticized for its lack of cohesion.

Eminem's lyrics on "Encore" were a particular point of contention among critics. While his storytelling abilities were still lauded, some felt that the content had become repetitive, rehashing themes from his previous albums without adding new insights. Others defended the lyrics as a natural continuation of Eminem's artistic journey.

The album's structure and pacing were frequently cited as weaknesses by critics. Many felt that at 20 tracks, "Encore" was overlong and would have benefited from more rigorous editing. The sequencing of serious tracks alongside more comedic ones was seen as jarring by some reviewers.

Some critics viewed "Encore" as a transitional album, seeing in it the signs of an artist struggling to evolve while maintaining the elements that had made him successful. This perspective led to more forgiving reviews that contextualized the album's flaws within Eminem's larger body of work.

The more personal tracks on "Encore," such as "Mockingbird" and "Like Toy Soldiers," generally received positive attention from critics. These songs were praised for their emotional depth and maturity, providing a counterpoint to the album's more controversial moments.

Comparisons to Eminem's previous work were inevitable in the critical discourse surrounding "Encore." While some reviewers felt the album didn't live up to the high standards set by "The Marshall Mathers LP" and "The Eminem Show," others appreciated it as a different kind of artistic statement.

The album's singles received particular scrutiny from critics. While "Mosh" was largely praised for its political engagement, "Just Lose It" was widely panned as a weak lead single that relied too heavily on cheap jokes and cultural references.

Some critics noted that the mixed quality of "Encore" might be attributed to Eminem's well-publicized personal struggles, particularly his increasing dependence on prescription drugs. This context led to more sympathetic readings of the album by some reviewers.

The critical reception of "Encore" sparked larger discussions about artistic evolution and the pressures faced by successful musicians. Many reviewers pondered whether Eminem could continue to innovate and surprise audiences after achieving such massive success with his earlier works.

Despite the mixed reviews, many critics maintained that even a subpar Eminem album contained moments of brilliance that most other rappers couldn't match. This backhanded compliment reflected Eminem's elevated status within the hip-hop world and the high expectations placed upon him.

The diversity of critical opinions on "Encore" reflected the album's polarizing nature. While it may not have achieved the consensus praise of his earlier works, it succeeded in provoking intense discussion and debate about Eminem's art and his place in popular culture.

6.3 Decision to Take a Break from Music

Following the release and mixed reception of "Encore," Eminem made the significant decision to step back from the music industry. This hiatus, which began in 2005, marked a crucial turning point in his career and personal life. The choice to retreat from the spotlight was driven by a complex interplay of factors, both professional and personal.

Eminem's struggles with prescription drug addiction had reached a critical point. The pressures of fame, coupled with the physical toll of touring and recording, had led to an increased reliance on sleep medication and painkillers. This dependency was affecting not only his health but also his creative output and personal relationships.

The relentless pace of Eminem's career since his breakthrough with "The Slim Shady LP" had left little time for self-reflection or personal growth. The rapper recognized the need to step away from the public eye to address his personal issues and reassess his artistic direction.

The mixed critical reception of "Encore" played a role in Eminem's decision to take a break. While the album was commercially successful, the lukewarm response from critics and some fans suggested that his formula might be growing stale. This realization likely contributed to his desire to regroup and refocus his creative energies.

Eminem's commitment to his role as a father also factored into his decision. The demands of his career had often conflicted with his desire to be present in his daughter Hailie's life. This hiatus offered an opportunity to prioritize his family relationships and provide a more stable environment for his children.

The constant scrutiny and controversy that surrounded Eminem had taken a toll on his mental health. The decision to step back from music provided a chance to escape the pressures of public life and find some measure of normalcy away from the spotlight.

Eminem's choice to take a break was also influenced by his desire to focus on other aspects of his career. During this period, he turned his attention to his record label, Shady Records, working to develop new artists and expand his business interests in the music industry.

The hiatus allowed Eminem to seek treatment for his substance abuse issues. He entered rehab in 2005, beginning a difficult but necessary journey towards sobriety. This process of recovery would profoundly impact both his personal life and his subsequent musical output.

CHAPTER 6

Eminem's decision to step back from music was met with a mix of concern and support from fans and industry insiders. While many worried about the future of his career, others recognized the importance of prioritizing health and well-being over continued commercial success.

The break from recording and performing gave Eminem the opportunity to reconnect with his roots in Detroit. He spent time in the city, reconnecting with old friends and collaborators, and rediscovering the inspirations that had fueled his early work.

During this hiatus, Eminem also took time to expand his horizons beyond music. He explored other creative outlets, including writing and producing for other artists. These experiences would later inform his approach to his own music when he returned to recording.

The death of his close friend and fellow rapper Proof in 2006 was a significant event during Eminem's hiatus. This tragic loss deepened Eminem's period of reflection and would later serve as a powerful influence on his music upon his return.

Eminem's retreat from the public eye sparked numerous rumors and speculations about his future in music. Some predicted that he had retired permanently, while others eagerly anticipated his eventual return. This period of uncertainty only served to heighten interest in his next moves.

The hiatus allowed Eminem to distance himself from the Slim Shady persona that had defined much of his early career. This break provided an opportunity to consider how he wanted to present himself as an artist moving forward, free from the expectations associated with his established image.

Eminem's decision to take a break also reflected broader trends in the music industry. Many artists who achieved massive success in the late 1990s and early 2000s found themselves taking similar hiatuses to recharge and reinvent themselves in the face of a rapidly changing musical landscape.

The time away from the spotlight allowed Eminem to process the whirlwind of fame he had experienced since his rise to stardom. This period of introspection would prove crucial in shaping the more mature and reflective tone of his later work.

Eminem's hiatus, while necessary for his personal well-being, also served to build anticipation for his eventual return to music. The break created a sense of mystery around the rapper, with fans and critics alike speculating about how his sound and subject matter might evolve during his time away.

CHAPTER 7

Personal Struggles and Comeback

7.1 Battles with Addiction

Eminem's battle with addiction became a defining aspect of his personal life and career during the mid-2000s. The rapper's dependence on prescription drugs, particularly sleep medication and painkillers, escalated to dangerous levels, threatening both his health and his artistic output.

The roots of Eminem's addiction can be traced back to the intense pressures of fame and the physical toll of his grueling work schedule. Insomnia, a common problem for the rapper, led to an initial reliance on sleep aids. This dependency gradually expanded to include various prescription painkillers, used to combat the physical strain of touring and performing.

Eminem's drug use began to noticeably affect his music and public appearances. Performances became erratic, and his once-sharp lyrics showed signs of diminished clarity. The rapper's weight fluctuated dramatically, and his overall health visibly declined, alarming fans and those close to him.

The death of Eminem's close friend and fellow D12 member, Proof, in 2006 exacerbated his substance abuse issues. Grief-stricken and struggling to cope, Eminem retreated further into drug use, using narcotics as a means of escaping the pain of loss and the pressures of his career.

Eminem's addiction reached a critical point in December 2007 when he suffered a methadone overdose. This near-fatal incident served as a wake-up call, forcing the rapper to confront the severity of his dependency and the urgent need for intervention.

Following the overdose, Eminem made the difficult decision to seek professional help. He entered a rehabilitation program, beginning the challenging process of detoxification and recovery. This period marked a turning point in both his personal life and his career trajectory.

The recovery process was far from easy for Eminem. He faced intense withdrawal symptoms and the daunting task of relearning how to function without the crutch of prescription drugs. The rapper's determination and the support of his loved ones played crucial roles in his ability to persevere through this challenging period.

Eminem's battle with addiction became a central theme in his music upon his return to recording. Songs like "Deja Vu" and "Going Through Changes" offered raw, unflinching accounts of his struggles with substance abuse, providing listeners with intimate insights into his journey towards sobriety.

The rapper's experiences with addiction and recovery profoundly impacted his worldview and artistic approach. His lyrics became more introspective and vulnerable, reflecting a newfound maturity and self-awareness born from his struggles.

Eminem's openness about his battles with addiction helped to destigmatize discussions about substance abuse within the hip-hop community and beyond. His willingness to share his experiences encouraged others facing similar challenges to seek help and fostered a more compassionate understanding of addiction.

The physical and mental toll of addiction and recovery left lasting impacts on Eminem. He had to relearn many basic skills, including how to rap and write lyrics without the influence of drugs. This process of rediscovery shaped the sound and content of his post-hiatus work.

Eminem's journey through addiction and towards recovery also affected his relationships, both personal and professional. Some friendships were strained or lost during his period of substance abuse, while others were strengthened through the recovery process. These changing dynamics influenced his support system and collaborative circles.

The rapper's struggles with addiction highlighted the darker side of fame and success in the music industry. Eminem's experiences shed light on the prevalence of substance abuse among artists and the need for better support systems within the entertainment world.

Eminem's battle with addiction became a cautionary tale for many in the hip-hop community. His near-death experience and subsequent recovery served as a powerful reminder of the dangers of drug abuse and the importance of seeking help when needed.

Throughout his recovery, Eminem developed new coping mechanisms to deal with stress and creative pressures. Exercise became a key part of his routine, helping him manage anxiety and maintain his physical health. These lifestyle changes played a crucial role in his ability to sustain his sobriety and reignite his career.

7.2 Divorce, Remarriage, and Family Issues

Eminem's personal life, particularly his relationships with his family, underwent significant turbulence during the mid-2000s. His tumultuous relationship with Kim Scott, his high school sweetheart and the mother of his daughter Hailie, continued to be a source of both inspiration and strife in his life and music.

The rapper's first marriage to Kim ended in divorce in 2001, following years of public feuds and personal struggles. However, the connection between them remained strong, leading to a remarriage in January 2006. This reunion was short-lived, with the couple divorcing again after just three months, in April of the same year.

The rapid cycle of remarriage and second divorce took a toll on Eminem's emotional well-being and contributed to his escalating substance abuse issues. The instability in his personal life was reflected in his music, with tracks from this period often exploring themes of love, betrayal, and the challenges of maintaining relationships in the public eye.

CHAPTER 7

Eminem's relationship with his daughter Hailie remained a central focus of his life throughout these personal struggles. His devotion to her was a recurring theme in his music, with songs like "Mockingbird" and "When I'm Gone" expressing his deep love for her and his anxieties about being a good father while navigating fame and personal demons.

The rapper's role as a father extended beyond his biological daughter. Eminem also took on the responsibility of raising his niece Alaina, whom he adopted, and Kim's daughter Whitney from a previous relationship. His commitment to providing a stable home for these children added another layer of complexity to his family dynamics.

Eminem's relationship with his own mother, Debbie Mathers, remained strained during this period. The two had a long history of public conflicts, often played out in Eminem's lyrics and his mother's media appearances. While attempts at reconciliation were made, their relationship continued to be a source of emotional turmoil for the rapper.

The death of Eminem's uncle and father figure, Ronnie Polkingharn, in 1991 continued to cast a long shadow over the rapper's life and relationships. Ronnie's suicide profoundly impacted Eminem, influencing his views on family, loyalty, and the fragility of life.

Eminem's fame and success created unique challenges for his family life. The constant media scrutiny and public interest in his personal affairs made it difficult to maintain privacy and normalcy for his children. Balancing his public persona with his role as a father became an ongoing struggle.

The rapper's battles with addiction further complicated his family relationships. His substance abuse issues strained his connections with loved ones and created an unstable environment for his children. The process of recovery and rebuilding trust became a crucial part of mending these familial bonds.

Eminem's experiences with family issues and relationship struggles became a central theme in his music. His lyrics often explored the complexities of love, the challenges of maintaining relationships in the spotlight, and the impact of his troubled past on his ability to form healthy connections.

The rapper's commitment to his family, particularly his children, played a significant role in his motivation to overcome his addiction and personal struggles. The desire to be a present and positive figure in their lives became a driving force in his recovery and career resurgence.

Eminem's family dynamics were further complicated by his status as a global celebrity. The contrast between his public image and his private role as a father and family man created internal conflicts that he often explored in his music.

The rapper's relationships with his D12 bandmates, whom he often referred to as his "family," were also affected by his personal struggles and periods of absence from the music scene. These friendships, particularly his bond with Proof, played a crucial role in both his personal life and his artistic development.

Eminem's experiences with family issues and relationship struggles resonated with many of his fans, who found solace and understanding in his honest portrayal of these challenges. His willingness to share his personal struggles helped to create a deeper connection with his audience.

The impact of Eminem's family issues extended beyond his personal life, influencing his business decisions and career trajectory. His desire to provide for his family and secure their future played a role in his various entrepreneurial ventures and his approach to managing his music career.

7.3 Return with Relapse in 2009

Eminem's return to the music scene with "Relapse" in 2009 marked a significant moment in his career, ending a nearly five-year hiatus. The album represented both a comeback and a reckoning, as the rapper grappled with his experiences of addiction, recovery, and personal turmoil through his music.

The creation of "Relapse" was a challenging process for Eminem. Relearning how to write and perform without the influence of drugs required him to essentially rebuild his creative process from the ground up. This struggle is reflected in the album's content, which often deals with themes of addiction, relapse, and the difficulties of maintaining sobriety.

Eminem's collaboration with Dr. Dre was crucial in the making of "Relapse." Dre's production provided a familiar foundation for Eminem to rebuild his confidence as an artist. The album's sound harkened back to their earlier collaborations while incorporating new elements that reflected Eminem's evolved artistic vision.

"Relapse" saw Eminem experimenting with different vocal styles and accents, a choice that divided critics and fans. This experimentation was partly a result of the rapper finding his voice again after years of substance abuse had affected his delivery. The accents also served as a form of artistic distancing, allowing Eminem to explore dark themes from a slightly removed perspective.

The album's lyrical content was notably dark, often delving into horrorcore territory. Tracks like "3 a.m." and "Stay Wide Awake" featured graphic imagery and disturbing narratives, reflecting the darker aspects of Eminem's psyche during his battles with addiction. This approach alienated some listeners while intriguing others with its raw, unfiltered exploration of the artist's inner demons.

"Relapse" also included more personal and introspective tracks. "Beautiful," written during the depths of Eminem's addiction, stood out as a poignant reflection on his struggles with self-esteem and mental health. This song provided a glimpse of the more mature, vulnerable artist that would emerge more fully in his subsequent work.

The album's lead single, "Crack a Bottle," featuring Dr. Dre and 50 Cent, broke the record for opening week download sales at the time. This commercial success demonstrated that despite his absence, Eminem's fan base remained strong and eager for new material.

Critical reception of "Relapse" was mixed. While many praised Eminem's technical skills and Dr. Dre's production, others found the album's content repetitive or overly shocking. The use of accents and the focus on horror-themed lyrics were particularly divisive elements among critics and fans alike.

"Relapse" debuted at number one on the Billboard 200 chart, selling

608,000 copies in its first week. This strong commercial performance confirmed Eminem's enduring popularity and his ability to connect with audiences even after a prolonged absence from the music scene.

The album's release was accompanied by a significant marketing campaign, including a series of online viral videos. These "Relapse" webisodes featured Eminem in a rehabilitation center, blending dark humor with promotion for the album. This marketing approach reflected the album's themes while generating buzz among fans.

Eminem's return with "Relapse" had a significant impact on the hip-hop landscape. His comeback reminded the industry of his influence and set the stage for a new phase in his career. The album reignited discussions about content and artistry in rap, with Eminem once again at the center of cultural debates.

The creation and release of "Relapse" served as a form of therapy for Eminem. The process of making the album allowed him to confront his past struggles and channel his experiences into his art. This cathartic aspect of the album was evident in its raw, often uncomfortable honesty.

"Relapse" featured fewer guest appearances than Eminem's previous albums, focusing more on his solo performance. This choice emphasized the personal nature of the album and Eminem's journey back to music. The few collaborations, such as "Crack a Bottle," served as strategic singles to help reintroduce Eminem to the charts.

The album's cover art, featuring a mosaic of Eminem's face made from pills, visually represented the central themes of addiction and recovery. This striking image became iconic, immediately conveying the album's subject matter and Eminem's personal struggles.

"Relapse" won Eminem a Grammy Award for Best Rap Album, his fifth win in this category. This recognition from the music industry validated his comeback and acknowledged the artistic merit of the album despite its controversial content.

The release of "Relapse" was followed by "Relapse: Refill," an expanded version of the album featuring seven new tracks. This re-release strategy kept Eminem in the public eye and provided fans with additional material, extending the album's impact and commercial life.

Eminem's return with "Relapse" set the stage for his continued evolution as an artist. While the album was in many ways a look back at his struggles, it also pointed toward a new chapter in his career. The honesty and vulnerability displayed in tracks like "Beautiful" hinted at the more mature, introspective direction his future work would take.

8

CHAPTER 8

Recovery and Reinvention

8.1 Release of Recovery in 2010

Eminem's seventh studio album, "Recovery," dropped on June 18, 2010, marking a significant turning point in his career. This release represented a stark departure from the darker themes and production style of "Relapse," showcasing a reinvigorated artist ready to confront his past and chart a new course.

The creation of "Recovery" began almost immediately after the completion of "Relapse." Initially conceived as a sequel titled "Relapse 2," the project evolved into something entirely different as Eminem found himself dissatisfied with the direction of the material. This dissatisfaction led to a complete overhaul of the album, resulting in "Recovery."

"Recovery" featured a noticeably different sound compared to Eminem's previous work. The rapper worked with a diverse group of producers, including Just Blaze, Jim Jonsin, and Boi-1da, moving away from his long-standing reliance on Dr. Dre's production. This shift in collaborators brought a fresh sonic palette to Eminem's music, incorporating more rock and pop elements into his hip-hop foundation.

Lyrically, "Recovery" saw Eminem at his most introspective and vulnerable. The album dealt candidly with his struggles with addiction, the challenges of recovery, and his determination to reclaim his life and career. This raw honesty resonated strongly with fans and critics alike, who praised Eminem's willingness to expose his flaws and insecurities.

The album's title, "Recovery," served as both a statement of intent and a reflection of Eminem's personal journey. It signaled to listeners that this was not just another album, but a testament to the rapper's renewed focus and commitment to his art and his life.

"Recovery" showcased Eminem's growth as an artist and a person. Gone were the shock tactics and violent imagery that had characterized much of his earlier work. In their place was a more mature, reflective lyrical approach that tackled serious themes with newfound depth and nuance.

The production on "Recovery" was notably more upbeat and anthemic compared to "Relapse." Tracks like "Not Afraid" and "Won't Back Down" featured soaring choruses and inspirational lyrics, reflecting Eminem's more positive mindset and his desire to connect with listeners on an emotional level.

Eminem's technical skills as a rapper remained as sharp as ever on "Recovery." His complex rhyme schemes and rapid-fire delivery were on full display, but now in service of more personal, introspective content. This combination of technical prowess and emotional depth set "Recovery" apart from much of Eminem's previous work.

The album featured several high-profile collaborations, including Pink, Rihanna, and Lil Wayne. These partnerships helped to broaden Eminem's appeal and demonstrated his willingness to step outside his comfort zone and engage with different styles and artists.

"Recovery" was released to significant commercial success, debuting at number one on the Billboard 200 chart and selling 741,000 copies in its first week. It went on to become the best-selling album of 2010 in the United States, cementing Eminem's comeback and proving his enduring popularity.

The album's cover art, featuring Eminem walking down a rural road, symbolized his journey of recovery and his forward-looking mindset. This simple yet powerful image reinforced the album's themes of personal growth and new beginnings.

"Recovery" marked a shift in Eminem's public persona. Interviews and appearances surrounding the album's release showed a more mature, reflective artist willing to acknowledge his past mistakes and discuss his struggles openly. This openness helped to humanize Eminem and deepen his connection with his audience.

The release of "Recovery" was accompanied by an extensive marketing campaign that leveraged both traditional media and emerging digital platforms. This multi-faceted approach helped to generate buzz around the album and reintroduce Eminem to a new generation of listeners.

"Recovery" represented not just a personal triumph for Eminem, but a creative rebirth. It proved that he could evolve as an artist, tackling new themes and styles while maintaining the core elements that had made him one of hip-hop's most influential figures.

The success of "Recovery" set the stage for the next phase of Eminem's career, establishing him as a mature artist capable of creating music that was both commercially successful and critically respected. It marked the beginning of a new chapter in his artistic journey, one characterized by introspection, growth, and a renewed sense of purpose.

8.2 Hit Singles "Not Afraid" and "Love the Way You Lie"

The release of "Recovery" was spearheaded by two massive hit singles that would come to define the album and this era of Eminem's career: "Not Afraid" and "Love the Way You Lie." These tracks not only dominated the charts but also showcased Eminem's artistic evolution and his ability to connect with a broad audience.

"Not Afraid," released as the lead single from "Recovery" on April 29, 2010, marked a significant departure from Eminem's previous work. The song's uplifting message and anthemic production signaled a new direction for the rapper, moving away from the darker themes that had characterized much of his earlier music.

Lyrically, "Not Afraid" served as a declaration of Eminem's commitment to sobriety and personal growth. The track's honest exploration of his struggles with addiction and his determination to overcome them resonated strongly with listeners. It became an anthem of perseverance, inspiring fans facing their own challenges.

The production of "Not Afraid," handled by Boi-1da, featured a powerful, rock-influenced instrumental that complemented Eminem's impassioned delivery. The track's soaring chorus and dramatic build-ups helped to make it an instant radio hit, appealing to listeners beyond Eminem's traditional hip-hop base.

"Not Afraid" debuted at number one on the Billboard Hot 100, making Eminem only the second artist in the chart's history to have a single debut at the top spot. This achievement underscored both the anticipation for new material from Eminem and the immediate impact of the song.

The music video for "Not Afraid," directed by Rich Lee, visually reinforced the song's themes of overcoming obstacles and personal growth. Shot in Newark, New Jersey, the video featured striking imagery of Eminem confronting his fears and literally taking a leap of faith, mirroring the song's message of courage in the face of adversity.

"Love the Way You Lie," featuring Rihanna, was released as the second single from "Recovery" on August 9, 2010. The track became one of the biggest hits of Eminem's career, topping charts worldwide and cementing his comeback.

The collaboration with Rihanna on "Love the Way You Lie" proved to be a masterstroke. The combination of Eminem's intense verses and Rihanna's haunting chorus created a powerful dynamic that captivated listeners. Their partnership brought together two of music's biggest stars, each bringing their own experiences and artistry to the track.

Lyrically, "Love the Way You Lie" explored the complex and often destructive nature of abusive relationships. Eminem's verses painted a vivid picture of a volatile partnership, while Rihanna's chorus captured the conflicted emotions of someone trapped in such a situation. The song's raw honesty and emotional depth struck a chord with millions of listeners.

The track's production, handled by Alex da Kid, featured a memorable guitar riff and a driving beat that perfectly complemented the song's intense subject matter. The polished pop production helped to make the song accessible to a wide audience while still maintaining Eminem's hip-hop credibility.

"Love the Way You Lie" spent seven weeks at number one on the Billboard Hot 100, becoming one of the best-selling singles of all time. Its success helped to drive sales of "Recovery" and solidified Eminem's position as one of the most commercially successful artists of his generation.

The music video for "Love the Way You Lie," directed by Joseph Kahn, starred actors Dominic Monaghan and Megan Fox in a visceral depiction of an abusive relationship. The video's unflinching portrayal of domestic violence sparked discussions about the song's message and its potential impact on viewers.

Both "Not Afraid" and "Love the Way You Lie" showcased Eminem's growth as an artist. These tracks demonstrated his ability to tackle serious subjects with nuance and depth, moving beyond the shock tactics of his earlier work to create music that was both commercially appealing and socially relevant.

The success of these singles played a crucial role in reestablishing Eminem as a dominant force in popular music. They proved that he

CHAPTER 8

could evolve his sound and subject matter while maintaining his core appeal, attracting new fans while satisfying his long-time followers.

These hit singles also highlighted Eminem's skill as a collaborator. While "Not Afraid" was a solo showcase, "Love the Way You Lie" demonstrated his ability to work effectively with other major artists, creating a sum greater than its parts. This collaborative success would influence Eminem's future work, leading to more high-profile partnerships.

The impact of "Not Afraid" and "Love the Way You Lie" extended beyond the charts. These songs became cultural touchstones, referenced and discussed in various media and social contexts. Their themes of personal struggle, redemption, and complex relationships resonated with a wide audience, cementing their place in popular culture.

Both singles received numerous award nominations and wins. "Love the Way You Lie" was nominated for Record of the Year and Song of the Year at the 53rd Grammy Awards, while "Not Afraid" won the Grammy for Best Rap Solo Performance. These accolades further validated Eminem's artistic comeback and the quality of his new material.

The massive success of these singles helped to redefine Eminem's public image. No longer just the controversial rapper of the early 2000s, he was now seen as a mature artist capable of creating music with broad appeal and meaningful content. This shift in perception opened up new opportunities for Eminem in terms of collaborations, endorsements, and public appearances.

8.3 Grammy Success and Critical Praise

The release of "Recovery" and its subsequent singles catapulted Eminem back into the spotlight of critical acclaim and industry recognition. The album's success at the Grammy Awards served as a powerful testament to Eminem's artistic resurgence and his ability to evolve as a musician.

At the 53rd Annual Grammy Awards in February 2011, "Recovery" won the award for Best Rap Album. This victory marked Eminem's sixth win in this category, extending his record as the artist with the most wins for Best Rap Album. The win underscored the album's impact on the hip-hop landscape and its significance within Eminem's discography.

"Recovery" was also nominated for Album of the Year, one of the most prestigious categories at the Grammy Awards. While it didn't win, the nomination itself was a significant acknowledgment of the album's quality and impact. It placed Eminem's work alongside the best music across all genres, highlighting his continued relevance and artistic merit.

Eminem's single "Not Afraid" won the Grammy for Best Rap Solo Performance. This win celebrated not only the song's commercial success but also its artistic achievement. The raw honesty and inspirational message of "Not Afraid" resonated with both the voting members of the Recording Academy and the general public.

"Love the Way You Lie," featuring Rihanna, received nominations for Record of the Year and Song of the Year. While it didn't win in these categories, the nominations themselves were a significant achievement, recognizing the song's massive cultural impact and its artistic qualities.

Eminem's performance at the Grammy ceremony further cemented his triumphant return. He delivered a powerful rendition of "Love the Way You Lie (Part II)" with Rihanna and Adam Levine, showcasing his live performance skills and the emotional depth of his new material.

The critical reception of "Recovery" was overwhelmingly positive, with many reviewers praising Eminem's artistic growth and the album's more mature themes. Critics appreciated the honesty and vulnerability displayed in the lyrics, seeing it as a welcome evolution from the shock tactics of his earlier work.

Many reviewers noted the album's more polished and diverse production, praising Eminem's willingness to experiment with new sounds and collaborators. The incorporation of rock and pop elements into his hip-hop foundation was seen as a successful artistic risk that paid off in terms of both critical and commercial success.

Eminem's technical skills as a rapper remained a point of universal praise. Critics marveled at his complex rhyme schemes, varied flow patterns, and clever wordplay, all of which were on full display throughout "Recovery." Many saw the album as a masterclass in rap technique, solidifying Eminem's status as one of the most skilled MCs in the game.

The emotional depth of "Recovery" was a frequent point of discussion in critical reviews. Many critics felt that Eminem had successfully translated his personal struggles into universally relatable music, creating an album that was both deeply personal and broadly appealing.

Eminem's collaborations on "Recovery," particularly "Love the Way You Lie" with Rihanna, received widespread acclaim. Critics praised his ability to work effectively with artists from different genres, creating crossover hits that appealed to a wide audience without compromising his artistic integrity.

The album's exploration of themes like addiction, recovery, and personal growth was seen as a mature and necessary evolution of Eminem's artistry. Many critics felt that this more introspective approach allowed Eminem to create some of the most powerful and affecting music of his career.

"Recovery" was featured on numerous "Best of 2010" lists compiled by music publications and critics. Its inclusion on these lists, often in high positions, further cemented its status as one of the year's most significant musical releases.

The critical and Grammy success of "Recovery" had a profound impact on Eminem's career trajectory. It reestablished him as a critical darling, proving that he could create music that was both commercially successful and artistically respected. This renewed critical acclaim opened doors for future collaborations and projects.

The praise for "Recovery" extended beyond music critics to include mental health professionals and addiction specialists. Many appreciated Eminem's honest portrayal of his struggles with substance abuse and the recovery process, seeing the album as a potential source of inspiration for others facing similar challenges.

The success of "Recovery" at the Grammys and in critical circles helped to elevate hip-hop's status within the mainstream music industry. Eminem's ability to create rap music that received recognition in major Grammy categories contributed to the ongoing legitimization of hip-hop as a respected art form.

CHAPTER 9

The Marshall Mathers LP 2

9.1 Announcement and Anticipation

The announcement of "The Marshall Mathers LP 2" in August 2013 sent shockwaves through the music industry and ignited a firestorm of excitement among Eminem's fanbase. The title alone, referencing his seminal 2000 album "The Marshall Mathers LP," set expectations sky-high and sparked intense speculation about the content and direction of this new project.

Eminem's decision to revisit the "Marshall Mathers LP" concept was a bold move that immediately raised questions about his artistic intentions. Fans and critics alike wondered how he would approach a sequel to such an iconic and controversial album, especially given his evolution as an artist in the intervening years.

EMINEM: THE VOICE OF A GENERATION

The announcement came in the form of a series of cryptic television commercials during the 2013 MTV Video Music Awards. These ads featured Eminem's signature blonde hair and hints of new music, cleverly building suspense and generating buzz without revealing too much information.

Social media exploded with reactions to the announcement, with fans dissecting every detail of the commercials and speculating about what the new album might sound like. The hashtag #MMLP2 quickly began trending worldwide, demonstrating the global anticipation for Eminem's new project.

Music industry insiders and commentators began to analyze the potential impact of "The Marshall Mathers LP 2" on Eminem's career and the broader hip-hop landscape. Many saw it as a high-risk, high-reward move that could either cement Eminem's legendary status or tarnish his legacy if it failed to live up to expectations.

The announcement of executive producers Dr. Dre and Rick Rubin further fueled excitement for the album. The combination of Dre's long-standing collaboration with Eminem and Rubin's legendary status in the music industry promised a unique and potentially groundbreaking sound for the project.

Eminem's relative silence in the immediate aftermath of the announcement only served to heighten the anticipation. His refusal to give interviews or provide details about the album's content left fans and media outlets hungry for any scraps of information they could find.

Speculation about potential guest features on the album ran rampant. Fans debated which artists might appear, with many hoping for reunions

CHAPTER 9

with past collaborators or dream matchups with contemporary stars.

The timing of the announcement, coming after the success of "Recovery" and Eminem's various guest appearances on other artists' tracks, positioned "The Marshall Mathers LP 2" as a potential career-defining moment. Many saw it as an opportunity for Eminem to solidify his status as one of hip-hop's all-time greats.

Music publications began to publish retrospectives on the original "Marshall Mathers LP," reexamining its impact and speculating on how its themes and style might be updated for a modern context. These articles helped to educate younger fans about the significance of the original album and build anticipation for its sequel.

Radio stations and music channels began to increase their play of Eminem's back catalog, particularly tracks from the original "Marshall Mathers LP." This renewed focus on his earlier work served to remind listeners of Eminem's artistic journey and set the stage for his new release.

Fan theories about the album's content began to circulate online, with some speculating that Eminem might revisit or update characters and storylines from the original "Marshall Mathers LP." These theories contributed to the buildup of anticipation and demonstrated the deep connection many fans felt to Eminem's work.

The announcement of "The Marshall Mathers LP 2" also reignited discussions about Eminem's place in the contemporary hip-hop landscape. With the rise of new stars and evolving styles within the genre, many were curious to see how Eminem would adapt his sound and themes to remain relevant.

Retailers began to prepare for what they anticipated would be one of the biggest album releases of the year. Pre-orders were made available, and marketing plans were put in place to capitalize on the expected high demand for the album.

The anticipation for "The Marshall Mathers LP 2" extended beyond just Eminem's music. Fans and media outlets speculated about potential music videos, live performances, and other promotional activities that might accompany the album's release.

9.2 Lead Single "Berzerk" and Album Release

The release of "Berzerk" as the lead single from "The Marshall Mathers LP 2" on August 27, 2013, marked the official kickoff of the album's campaign. The track, produced by Rick Rubin, immediately caught listeners' attention with its old-school hip-hop sound and rock influences, signaling a new direction for Eminem's music.

"Berzerk" featured a sample from Billy Squier's "The Stroke," along with elements from the Beastie Boys' "The New Style," creating a nostalgic yet fresh sound that paid homage to hip-hop's roots. This production choice demonstrated Eminem's willingness to experiment with different styles and his respect for the genre's history.

Lyrically, "Berzerk" showcased Eminem's trademark wordplay and pop culture references. The song's high-energy delivery and irreverent tone harkened back to the spirit of his earlier work, particularly the original "Marshall Mathers LP," while still feeling contemporary and relevant.

The music video for "Berzerk," directed by Syndrome, featured cameo

CHAPTER 9

appearances from Kid Rock, Kendrick Lamar, and Rick Rubin. The video's retro aesthetic, complete with VHS-style effects, complemented the song's old-school vibe and added a visual dimension to the track's nostalgic elements.

"Berzerk" debuted at number three on the Billboard Hot 100 chart, Eminem's highest debut since "Love the Way You Lie" in 2010. This strong commercial performance demonstrated that Eminem's popularity remained undiminished and built further anticipation for the full album release.

The single's success on rock-oriented radio stations, in addition to its performance on hip-hop and Top 40 formats, highlighted Eminem's cross-genre appeal. This broad reach helped to expand the potential audience for "The Marshall Mathers LP 2."

Following the release of "Berzerk," Eminem began a more active promotional campaign for the album. This included interviews, television appearances, and live performances, each of which provided new insights into the album's creation and themes.

The album's track list was revealed on October 10, 2013, featuring collaborations with Rihanna, Kendrick Lamar, Nate Ruess, and Skylar Grey. This diverse lineup of guest artists hinted at the album's musical variety and Eminem's continued willingness to work with both established stars and rising talents.

On November 5, 2013, "The Marshall Mathers LP 2" was officially released. The album's arrival was met with intense interest from fans and critics alike, many of whom were eager to see how Eminem had approached the concept of a sequel to his iconic 2000 release.

The album's cover art, featuring Eminem's childhood home in Detroit, created a visual link to the original "Marshall Mathers LP" and emphasized the personal nature of the project. This imagery reinforced the album's themes of revisiting the past and reflecting on Eminem's journey as an artist and individual.

Deluxe editions of the album included additional tracks, providing fans with extra content and incentivizing purchases of physical copies in an era of digital streaming. These bonus tracks often explored themes and styles that complemented the main album while standing as worthy additions to Eminem's catalog.

The release was accompanied by a series of music videos for key tracks, each adding visual context to the album's themes and showcasing Eminem's continued creativity in this medium. These videos helped to maintain momentum for the album in the weeks following its initial release.

Eminem embarked on a series of high-profile live performances to promote the album, including appearances on Saturday Night Live and the MTV Europe Music Awards. These performances allowed him to showcase the new material in a live setting and demonstrate his enduring skills as a performer.

The release of "The Marshall Mathers LP 2" was a global event, with simultaneous launches in multiple countries. This coordinated international release strategy highlighted Eminem's status as a global superstar and ensured that fans worldwide could experience the album at the same time.

Fan reaction to the album was immediate and intense, with social media platforms flooded with discussions, reviews, and reactions to the new material. This online buzz helped to drive both streams and sales of the album in its crucial first weeks of release.

9.3 Critical Reception and Commercial Performance

The critical reception of "The Marshall Mathers LP 2" was largely positive, with many reviewers praising Eminem's technical skills and the album's ambitious scope. Critics noted the project's ties to the original "Marshall Mathers LP" while acknowledging its distinct identity as a modern hip-hop album.

Many reviews highlighted Eminem's lyrical dexterity, with particular praise given to tracks like "Rap God," which showcased his ability to deliver complex rhyme schemes at breakneck speeds. This track became a talking point for critics, with many citing it as evidence of Eminem's continued dominance as a technical rapper.

The album's production, helmed by a mix of longtime collaborators and new partners, received generally positive feedback. Critics appreciated the diverse sonic palette, which ranged from the rock-influenced "Berzerk" to more traditional hip-hop beats. The involvement of Rick Rubin was frequently noted as a positive influence on the album's sound.

Some reviewers drew comparisons between "The Marshall Mathers LP 2" and its predecessor, noting both similarities and differences. While some felt the album successfully captured the spirit of the original, others argued that it stood as its own entity, reflecting Eminem's growth as an artist over the intervening years.

The album's more introspective tracks, such as "Headlights," which addressed Eminem's relationship with his mother, were singled out for praise. Many critics saw these moments of vulnerability as evidence of Eminem's maturation as both an artist and a person.

Commercial performance of "The Marshall Mathers LP 2" was strong from the outset. The album debuted at number one on the Billboard 200 chart, selling 792,000 copies in its first week. This marked Eminem's seventh consecutive number-one album in the United States, a testament to his enduring popularity.

Internationally, the album achieved similar success, topping charts in numerous countries including the United Kingdom, Canada, and Australia. This global performance underscored Eminem's status as an international superstar and the universal appeal of his music.

The album's singles performed well on various charts. "The Monster," featuring Rihanna, became a particular standout, reaching number one on the Billboard Hot 100 and achieving similar success in other countries. This collaboration further cemented Eminem and Rihanna's status as a powerhouse musical duo.

"The Marshall Mathers LP 2" was certified double platinum by the RIAA less than three months after its release, signifying sales of over two million units in the United States. This rapid certification highlighted the album's commercial appeal and Eminem's ability to move units in an era of declining album sales.

The album's success extended to the streaming realm, with tracks from "The Marshall Mathers LP 2" accumulating millions of plays on platforms like Spotify and Apple Music. This digital performance

CHAPTER 9

demonstrated Eminem's ability to connect with younger, streaming-oriented listeners while maintaining his traditional sales base.

Critical discussions of the album often centered on its place within Eminem's discography. Many reviewers saw it as a return to form after the more pop-oriented "Recovery," while others viewed it as a natural evolution of his style. These debates contributed to the album's cultural impact and kept it in the public conversation long after its release.

The album received numerous award nominations, including a Grammy nomination for Best Rap Album. While it didn't win in this category, the nomination itself was seen as recognition of the album's quality and impact.

Some critics noted that while the album was strong overall, it occasionally suffered from inconsistency. Certain tracks were singled out as weaker links, with a few reviewers arguing that the album could have benefited from tighter editing.

The album's exploration of Eminem's past, both lyrically and through its connection to the original "Marshall Mathers LP," was a frequent topic of critical discussion. Many saw this self-reflection as a strength, providing depth and context to Eminem's current artistic identity.

Comparisons to contemporary hip-hop artists were common in reviews of "The Marshall Mathers LP 2." Critics often positioned Eminem in relation to younger rappers, with many arguing that the album proved he could still compete with and even surpass newer artists in terms of skill and creativity.

The album's commercial and critical success helped to solidify Eminem's legacy as one of hip-hop's most enduring and influential figures. It demonstrated his ability to remain relevant and compelling well into his forties, a rare feat in a genre often associated with youth culture.

Long-term, "The Marshall Mathers LP 2" has maintained its standing as a significant entry in Eminem's catalog. Its blend of technical prowess, introspection, and nods to hip-hop history has ensured its place in discussions of 2010s hip-hop, cementing its status as a notable release of the decade.

CHAPTER 10

Collaborations and Reunions

10.1 Work with D12 and Royce 5'9"

Eminem's collaborations with D12 and Royce 5'9" represent significant chapters in his career, showcasing his loyalty to long-time friends and his roots in Detroit's hip-hop scene. These partnerships have produced some of the most memorable moments in Eminem's discography and have played a crucial role in shaping his artistic identity.

D12, the hip-hop collective formed in Detroit in the mid-1990s, has been an integral part of Eminem's musical journey. The group's first mainstream success came with the album "Devil's Night" in 2001, which featured Eminem prominently and capitalized on his rising stardom. Tracks like "Purple Pills" and "Fight Music" became instant hits, blending the group's raw energy with Eminem's razor-sharp lyricism.

The tragic death of D12 member Proof in 2006 had a profound impact on both the group and Eminem personally. Proof had been a close friend and mentor to Eminem, and his loss created a void that was felt deeply in their music and personal lives. This event led to a period of reflection and regrouping for both Eminem and D12.

In subsequent years, Eminem continued to work with the remaining members of D12 on various projects. The group's 2004 album "D12 World" showcased their evolving sound and Eminem's growing influence as a producer. While not as commercially successful as their debut, it demonstrated the group's continued relevance in the hip-hop landscape.

Eminem's solo work often featured appearances from D12 members, keeping the group's spirit alive even as they pursued individual projects. These collaborations served as a reminder of Eminem's roots and his commitment to supporting his long-time associates.

The relationship between Eminem and Royce 5'9" has been one of hip-hop's most intriguing narratives. Initially collaborating as the duo Bad Meets Evil in the late 1990s, their partnership produced the underground hit "Scary Movies." However, tensions between Royce and D12 led to a falling out with Eminem, resulting in years of estrangement.

The reconciliation between Eminem and Royce in 2011 marked a significant moment in both of their careers. This reunion led to the release of the EP "Hell: The Sequel" under the Bad Meets Evil moniker. The project was met with critical acclaim and commercial success, demonstrating the enduring chemistry between the two MCs.

"Hell: The Sequel" showcased Eminem and Royce's complementary styles, with both rappers pushing each other to new heights of technical proficiency and lyrical creativity. Tracks like "Fast Lane" and "Lighters" became fan favorites, blending intricate wordplay with catchy hooks.

The renewed partnership between Eminem and Royce extended beyond their Bad Meets Evil project. Royce became a frequent collaborator on Eminem's solo work and was signed to Shady Records as part of the group Slaughterhouse. This multi-faceted relationship allowed both artists to support and influence each other's careers in various ways.

Eminem's work with both D12 and Royce 5'9" has been characterized by a sense of artistic growth and mutual respect. These collaborations have allowed Eminem to explore different aspects of his musical personality, from the more playful and outrageous style of D12 to the technically intricate and lyrically dense approach of his work with Royce.

The influence of these collaborations on Eminem's solo work is evident in his continued emphasis on complex rhyme schemes and his willingness to engage in friendly competition with his fellow MCs. The spirit of one-upmanship that characterizes much of his work with D12 and Royce has pushed Eminem to constantly refine and evolve his craft.

These partnerships have also played a significant role in maintaining Eminem's connection to the Detroit hip-hop scene. By continuing to work with local artists and support homegrown talent, Eminem has helped to keep Detroit on the map as a major hub of hip-hop culture and creativity.

The legacy of Eminem's work with D12 and Royce 5'9" extends beyond the music itself. These collaborations have become an integral part of hip-hop lore, representing the power of loyalty, reconciliation, and artistic kinship in a genre often characterized by rivalry and conflict.

Eminem's ongoing relationships with D12 and Royce 5'9" serve as a testament to his commitment to his roots and his belief in the power of collaboration. These partnerships have not only produced great music but have also helped to shape Eminem's identity as an artist who values long-standing relationships and artistic growth.

10.2 Shady Records and Fostering New Talent

Shady Records, founded by Eminem and his manager Paul Rosenberg in 1999, has played a crucial role in shaping the landscape of hip-hop over the past two decades. The label has served as a platform for Eminem to support and develop new talent, while also extending his influence beyond his own music.

The early years of Shady Records saw the label signing and promoting artists closely associated with Eminem. D12 was one of the first acts signed to the label, with their debut album "Devil's Night" marking Shady Records' first release outside of Eminem's solo work. This set the tone for the label as a home for artists within Eminem's inner circle.

The signing of 50 Cent in 2002 marked a turning point for Shady Records. Eminem's support and mentorship played a crucial role in 50 Cent's rise to superstardom. The massive success of 50 Cent's debut album "Get Rich or Die Tryin'" not only launched a new hip-hop icon but also established Shady Records as a major player in the industry.

Eminem's approach to running Shady Records has been characterized

CHAPTER 10

by a hands-on mentorship style. He has been known to work closely with the label's artists, offering guidance on everything from lyrical content to delivery and stage presence. This personal investment in the development of new talent has become a hallmark of the Shady Records brand.

The label's roster has evolved over the years, reflecting changes in the hip-hop landscape and Eminem's own artistic interests. Artists like Obie Trice, Stat Quo, and Bobby Creekwater were early signings that helped to establish the label's sound and identity.

Shady Records' signing of Slaughterhouse in 2011 represented a shift towards more lyrically-focused, hardcore hip-hop. The group, consisting of Joe Budden, Joell Ortiz, Royce 5'9", and KXNG CROOKED, aligned closely with Eminem's own emphasis on technical skill and complex lyricism.

The label has also served as a platform for Eminem to explore his interests as a producer and executive. His involvement in the careers of Shady Records artists has allowed him to influence the direction of hip-hop beyond his own music, shaping the sound and style of a new generation of rappers.

Shady Records has faced challenges over the years, including changing market dynamics and the evolving tastes of hip-hop audiences. The label has had to adapt to the rise of streaming and social media, finding new ways to promote and develop artists in the digital age.

The label's commitment to artistic integrity has sometimes come at the cost of commercial success. While some Shady Records artists have achieved mainstream popularity, others have remained more niche, appealing to hardcore hip-hop fans rather than a broader audience.

Eminem's own evolution as an artist has been reflected in the changing roster and focus of Shady Records. As he has matured and his interests have shifted, the label has similarly adapted, signing artists that align with his current artistic vision.

The legacy of Shady Records extends beyond the artists it has signed. The label has played a significant role in preserving and promoting a certain style of hip-hop, characterized by technical proficiency, complex lyricism, and a respect for the genre's roots.

Shady Records has also served as a model for other artist-led labels in hip-hop. Eminem's success in balancing his own career with the development of new talent has inspired other established artists to launch their own imprints.

The future of Shady Records remains closely tied to Eminem's vision and involvement. While the label has experienced periods of quiet, it continues to be a force in hip-hop, with the potential to launch new stars and shape the direction of the genre.

Eminem's role as a label head has added another dimension to his legacy in hip-hop. Beyond his own music, his work in discovering and nurturing new talent has ensured that his influence will be felt in the genre for years to come.

The story of Shady Records is ultimately one of Eminem's commitment to hip-hop culture and his desire to give back to the genre that made him a star. Through the label, he has created opportunities for both established and up-and-coming artists, helping to ensure the continued vitality and evolution of hip-hop.

10.3 High-Profile Collaborations Across Genres

Eminem's willingness to collaborate with artists across various genres has been a defining characteristic of his later career, demonstrating his versatility and broadening his appeal beyond the traditional hip-hop audience. These high-profile collaborations have resulted in some of the most commercially successful and critically acclaimed tracks of his career.

One of the most notable collaborations in Eminem's catalog is his work with pop star Rihanna. Their first track together, "Love the Way You Lie" from the album "Recovery," became a global smash hit, topping charts worldwide and earning critical praise for its raw emotional content. The success of this collaboration led to further team-ups, including "The Monster" from "The Marshall Mathers LP 2," which achieved similar commercial success.

Eminem's partnership with singer-songwriter Skylar Grey has produced several notable tracks. Grey, who co-wrote "Love the Way You Lie," has featured on multiple Eminem songs, including "I Need a Doctor" (also featuring Dr. Dre) and "Asshole" from "The Marshall Mathers LP 2." Their collaborations often blend Eminem's intense rapping with Grey's ethereal vocals, creating a unique and compelling sound.

The rapper's work with rock artists has allowed him to explore different sonic territories. His collaboration with Aerosmith on a remixed version of "Sing for the Moment," which sampled the band's "Dream

On," bridged the gap between hip-hop and classic rock. Similarly, his feature on Pink's "Won't Back Down" showcased his ability to adapt his style to a more rock-oriented track.

Eminem's collaborations have also extended to the world of pop music. His feature on Nicki Minaj's "Roman's Revenge" demonstrated his ability to go toe-to-toe with one of hip-hop's most dynamic female MCs. Meanwhile, his work with Ed Sheeran on "River" showed his willingness to venture into more melodic, pop-oriented territory.

The rapper's collaboration with Beyoncé on "Walk On Water," the lead single from his album "Revival," was seen as a meeting of two music industry titans. The track's stripped-back production allowed both artists' vocals to shine, creating an intimate and introspective piece that diverged from Eminem's typically more aggressive style.

Eminem's work with fellow rappers from different eras and styles has produced some of his most interesting collaborations. His feature on Drake's "Forever," alongside Kanye West and Lil Wayne, was seen as a summit meeting of hip-hop's biggest names. Similarly, his collaboration with Kendrick Lamar on "Love Game" brought together two of the genre's most technically skilled MCs.

The rapper's willingness to work with younger artists has helped him stay relevant in an ever-changing musical landscape. His feature on Joyner Lucas's "Lucky You" showcased his ability to adapt to more contemporary rap styles, while his collaboration with Juice WRLD on "Godzilla" demonstrated his influence on a new generation of hip-hop artists.

Eminem's collaborations have not been limited to musical artists. His work on the soundtrack for the film "Venom," including the title track, showed his ability to create music that complements visual media. This venture into film soundtracks opened up new avenues for his music to reach audiences.

The rapper's collaborative work has often allowed him to explore themes and styles that diverge from his solo material. These partnerships have provided opportunities for Eminem to show different facets of his artistry, from vulnerability in ballads to playfulness in more upbeat tracks.

Eminem's high-profile collaborations have played a significant role in maintaining his commercial viability. Many of these tracks have become hit singles, helping to keep him in the public eye and on the charts between album releases.

These collaborations have also served to broaden Eminem's fan base. By working with artists from different genres, he has been able to reach listeners who might not typically engage with his music, thereby expanding his audience and influence.

The diverse nature of Eminem's collaborations reflects the increasing genre fluidity in popular music. His willingness to cross genre boundaries has contributed to the broader trend of hybridization in contemporary music, where elements of hip-hop, pop, rock, and other genres freely intermingle.

Eminem's collaborative works have often provided a platform for him to address different themes or adopt different personas than he typically does in his solo work. This has allowed him to explore new creative territories and keep his artistry fresh and evolving.

The success of these high-profile collaborations has cemented Eminem's status as not just a hip-hop icon, but a true pop culture phenomenon. His ability to work effectively with such a wide range of artists speaks to his versatility and enduring relevance in the music industry.

CHAPTER 11

Eminem's Acting Career

11.1 Starring Role in 8 Mile

Eminem's transition from rapper to actor reached its pinnacle with his starring role in the 2002 film "8 Mile." The semi-autobiographical drama, directed by Curtis Hanson, marked Eminem's debut as a lead actor and proved to be a critical and commercial success.

The film's story, while fictionalized, drew heavily from Eminem's own experiences growing up in Detroit. Set in 1995, "8 Mile" follows Jimmy "B-Rabbit" Smith Jr., a young white rapper trying to launch his career in Detroit's predominantly African American hip-hop scene. The parallels between Jimmy's journey and Eminem's own rise to fame provided a sense of authenticity that resonated with audiences.

Eminem's performance in "8 Mile" surprised many critics who had been skeptical of his acting abilities. He brought a raw, unpolished energy to the role that perfectly captured Jimmy's struggles and ambitions. His portrayal was praised for its honesty and emotional depth, with many noting that Eminem seemed to be channeling his own experiences into the character.

The film's depiction of Detroit's hip-hop underground was particularly noteworthy. Eminem's insider knowledge of this world helped to create a vivid and authentic portrayal of the battle rap scene. The rap battles featured in the film became some of its most memorable moments, showcasing Eminem's lyrical prowess and ability to perform under pressure.

"8 Mile" also explored themes of class struggle, racial tensions, and the power of art as a means of escape. Through Jimmy's story, the film touched on issues of poverty, broken families, and the challenges faced by those trying to break out of their circumstances. These themes gave the film a depth that went beyond a simple rags-to-riches story.

The supporting cast of "8 Mile" complemented Eminem's performance well. Kim Basinger's portrayal of Jimmy's mother added emotional weight to the story, while Mekhi Phifer and Brittany Murphy brought energy and charm to their roles as Jimmy's friends and supporters.

The film's production design and cinematography effectively captured the gritty, industrial atmosphere of mid-90s Detroit. This visual aesthetic contributed significantly to the film's mood and helped to immerse viewers in Jimmy's world.

"8 Mile" was a box office success, grossing over $240 million worldwide. Its commercial performance demonstrated Eminem's star power and ability to draw audiences beyond his usual fan base. The film's success also helped to further legitimize hip-hop culture in mainstream cinema.

Critically, "8 Mile" was well-received. Many reviewers praised the film for its authentic portrayal of the Detroit rap scene and its compelling underdog story. Eminem's performance, in particular, was singled out for praise, with some critics suggesting that he had genuine potential as an actor.

The film's impact extended beyond the cinema. It sparked renewed interest in battle rap and freestyle competitions, influencing a new generation of aspiring MCs. The film's depiction of this aspect of hip-hop culture helped to bring it to a wider audience.

"8 Mile" also had a significant impact on Eminem's public image. The film humanized him in the eyes of many, providing context for his often controversial public persona. It allowed audiences to see a more vulnerable side of the rapper, contributing to a broader understanding of his artistry and background.

The success of "8 Mile" opened up new possibilities for Eminem's career. It demonstrated his ability to carry a film and suggested that he could potentially have a future in acting if he chose to pursue it. However, Eminem would ultimately decide to focus primarily on his music career, making "8 Mile" a unique entry in his filmography.

The film's soundtrack, featuring new material from Eminem, became a massive hit in its own right. The album's success further amplified the impact of the film and provided Eminem with some of the biggest hits of his career.

"8 Mile" remains a significant cultural touchstone, often cited as one of the best hip-hop films ever made. Its influence can be seen in subsequent films about rap and urban culture, many of which have tried to capture the gritty realism and authenticity that made "8 Mile" so compelling.

The film's legacy in Eminem's career is substantial. It represents a moment when he successfully crossed over into a new medium, expanding his artistic range and cementing his status as a multi-faceted entertainer. While he would not pursue acting as actively in the years that followed, "8 Mile" stands as a testament to his abilities beyond music.

11.2 "Lose Yourself" and Oscar Victory

The creation and subsequent success of "Lose Yourself," the lead single from the "8 Mile" soundtrack, marked a pivotal moment in Eminem's career. The track not only became one of his most iconic songs but also earned him an Academy Award, a first for a rap artist in the Best Original Song category.

Eminem wrote "Lose Yourself" during breaks while filming "8 Mile," often jotting down lyrics on a sheet of paper or a napkin between takes. This unconventional writing process contributed to the raw, urgent quality of the lyrics, which capture the pressure and determination of an aspiring rapper preparing for a crucial performance.

The song's production, handled by Eminem himself along with longtime collaborators Jeff Bass and Luis Resto, featured a driving guitar riff and intense drum pattern that perfectly complemented the motivational tone of the lyrics. The track's rock-influenced sound helped it appeal

CHAPTER 11

to listeners beyond Eminem's usual hip-hop audience.

Lyrically, "Lose Yourself" encapsulates the central themes of "8 Mile," serving as both a character study of Jimmy "B-Rabbit" Smith Jr. and a broader anthem of perseverance in the face of adversity. The song's opening lines, "His palms are sweaty, knees weak, arms are heavy," have become some of the most recognized in hip-hop history.

The track's chorus, with its exhortation to "lose yourself in the music, the moment, you own it," resonated strongly with listeners. Its message of seizing opportunities and overcoming self-doubt struck a chord that extended far beyond the context of the film, turning "Lose Yourself" into a universal motivational anthem.

Upon its release, "Lose Yourself" became an immediate commercial success. The song spent 12 weeks at number one on the Billboard Hot 100, becoming Eminem's first chart-topping single in the United States. Its popularity extended globally, with the track reaching number one in numerous countries.

Critical reception for "Lose Yourself" was overwhelmingly positive. Music critics praised the song's intensity, its narrative structure, and Eminem's passionate delivery. Many noted that the track represented a new level of maturity in Eminem's songwriting, moving beyond the shock tactics of his earlier work to create something more universally relatable.

The music video for "Lose Yourself," which intercut scenes from "8 Mile" with footage of Eminem performing the song, further amplified its impact. The video's gritty aesthetic and intense energy perfectly captured the spirit of both the song and the film.

"Lose Yourself" earned Eminem an Academy Award for Best Original Song at the 75th Academy Awards in 2003. This victory was historic, marking the first time a rap song had won in this category. The win further legitimized hip-hop in the eyes of the mainstream entertainment industry.

Eminem's absence from the Oscar ceremony became almost as notable as the win itself. The rapper, who was reportedly napping at home during the awards, later expressed regret at not attending to accept the award in person.

The Oscar win for "Lose Yourself" had a significant impact on Eminem's career and public image. It elevated him from a controversial rapper to an acclaimed songwriter, earning him respect from corners of the entertainment industry that had previously been skeptical of his talent.

In the years following its release, "Lose Yourself" has become one of Eminem's most enduring tracks. It regularly features on lists of the greatest hip-hop songs of all time and has been used in numerous films, TV shows, and advertisements, often to evoke feelings of determination and triumph over adversity.

The song's legacy extends beyond music into the realm of sports and motivation. "Lose Yourself" has become a popular choice for athletes' warm-up playlists and is often played at sporting events to energize crowds. Its message of giving your all when opportunity knocks has resonated in a variety of contexts.

"Lose Yourself" has also had a lasting impact on hip-hop production. Its use of rock elements, particularly the prominent guitar riff, influenced a trend of genre-blending in hip-hop that continues to this day.

CHAPTER 11

The track's success opened up new avenues for hip-hop artists in film. It demonstrated that rap could produce not just popular songs but critically acclaimed, award-winning compositions, paving the way for greater integration of hip-hop in film soundtracks.

"Lose Yourself" remains a high point in Eminem's discography, a song that transcended its origins as a film soundtrack to become a cultural touchstone. Its success at the Oscars helped to bridge the gap between hip-hop and mainstream entertainment, contributing to the genre's growing acceptance in all corners of popular culture.

11.3 Other Film and Television Appearances

While "8 Mile" stands as Eminem's most significant foray into acting, his career has included several other notable film and television appearances. These roles, ranging from cameos to voice acting, have allowed Eminem to showcase different facets of his personality and talent beyond his music career.

Eminem's first appearance on the big screen came in 2001 with a brief cameo in "The Wash," a comedy starring Dr. Dre and Snoop Dogg. Although his role was minor, it hinted at his potential for screen presence and his willingness to venture into acting.

In 2009, Eminem made a memorable appearance in the comedy film "Funny People," starring Adam Sandler and directed by Judd Apatow. Playing himself, Eminem delivered a deadpan, self-deprecating performance that surprised many with its comedic timing. This cameo showcased a different side of the rapper, demonstrating his ability to poke fun at his public image.

Eminem's voice acting debut came in 2010 with an appearance on the animated series "Entourage." Again playing himself, he showed his versatility by translating his personality to a voice-only performance. This appearance helped to keep him in the public eye during a relatively quiet period in his music career.

The rapper's most substantial role post-"8 Mile" came in the 2014 film "The Interview," starring James Franco and Seth Rogen. In a brief but impactful scene, Eminem deadpans that he's gay, playing on the controversies surrounding his lyrics and public statements about homosexuality. This appearance demonstrated his willingness to engage with and subvert public perceptions of his persona.

Eminem has also made several appearances on television talk shows, often participating in skits or segments that showcase his dry wit and self-awareness. His 2009 appearance at the MTV Movie Awards, where he appeared to be offended by Sacha Baron Cohen's Bruno character landing on him, created a viral moment that kept people talking for weeks.

In 2017, Eminem appeared in the HBO documentary series "The Defiant Ones," which chronicled the partnership between Dr. Dre and Jimmy Iovine. His interviews provided valuable insights into his relationship with Dr. Dre and his early career, adding depth to the documentary's exploration of hip-hop history.

Eminem's music has been featured prominently in numerous films and TV shows, even when he doesn't appear on screen. His songs have become shorthand for intensity, determination, or edgy humor in visual media, further cementing his place in popular culture.

CHAPTER 11

The rapper has also been involved in producing for television. In 2017, he served as an executive producer on the battle rap competition series "One Shot," leveraging his credibility in the hip-hop world to bring authenticity to the show.

Eminem's appearances in documentaries about hip-hop and music history have helped to contextualize his place in the genre. His thoughtful reflections on his career and the evolution of hip-hop have added valuable perspective to these historical overviews.

While Eminem hasn't taken on another major acting role since "8 Mile," his selective appearances in film and television have helped to maintain his presence in popular culture beyond music. These cameos and small roles have allowed him to play with his public image, often subverting expectations.

Eminem's venture into film production came with the 2017 battle rap film "Bodied," which he produced. While he didn't appear in the film, his involvement helped to bring attention to the project and demonstrated his ongoing commitment to supporting and showcasing battle rap culture.

The rapper's music videos have often blurred the line between music and short film, with elaborate narratives and high production values. Videos like "Stan" and "Space Bound" showcase Eminem's comfort in front of the camera and his ability to convey complex emotions through acting.

Eminem's performance of "Lose Yourself" at the 92nd Academy Awards in 2020, 17 years after the song won an Oscar, was a surprise highlight of the ceremony. This appearance reminded audiences of his impact on both music and film, bridging his past achievements with his ongoing relevance.

Throughout his career, Eminem has been the subject of numerous unauthorized documentaries and biopics. While not directly involved in these projects, they speak to the enduring fascination with his life story and his impact on popular culture.

Eminem's selective approach to film and television appearances has helped to maintain an air of mystique around him. By choosing his roles carefully and often playing versions of himself, he has managed to engage with visual media without compromising his primary identity as a musician.

CHAPTER 12

Business Ventures and Philanthropy

12.1 Shady Records and Music Production

Eminem's business acumen extends far beyond his success as a recording artist. The establishment of Shady Records in 1999, in partnership with his manager Paul Rosenberg, marked Eminem's foray into the business side of the music industry. This venture has allowed him to shape the careers of other artists and leave an indelible mark on hip-hop beyond his own music.

Shady Records' first major success came with the signing of D12, Eminem's Detroit-based rap group. The label's support helped propel D12's debut album, "Devil's Night," to multi-platinum status, establishing Shady Records as a force to be reckoned with in the industry.

The signing of 50 Cent in 2002 proved to be a watershed moment for

Shady Records. Eminem's mentorship and the label's backing played a crucial role in 50 Cent's rise to superstardom. The massive success of "Get Rich or Die Tryin'" not only launched 50 Cent's career but also cemented Shady Records' reputation for identifying and nurturing top-tier talent.

Over the years, Shady Records has been home to a diverse roster of artists, including Obie Trice, Stat Quo, Bobby Creekwater, and Cashis. While not all of these artists achieved the same level of success as 50 Cent, they contributed to the label's reputation for signing skilled lyricists and authentic hip-hop artists.

The label's signing of Slaughterhouse in 2011 represented a shift towards more lyrically-focused, hardcore hip-hop. This move aligned closely with Eminem's own emphasis on technical skill and complex lyricism, reinforcing the label's commitment to "real" hip-hop in an era of increasingly pop-oriented rap.

Eminem's role at Shady Records goes beyond just signing artists. He has been actively involved in the production and creative direction of many of the label's releases. His hands-on approach has helped to shape the sound and style of Shady Records' output, ensuring a level of quality and consistency across the label's releases.

The label has faced challenges over the years, including changing market dynamics and evolving tastes in hip-hop. Shady Records has had to adapt to the rise of streaming and social media, finding new ways to promote and develop artists in the digital age.

Eminem's production work, both for Shady Records artists and others, has been an important aspect of his business ventures in music. He

CHAPTER 12

has produced tracks for a wide range of artists, from long-time collaborators like Dr. Dre to newer acts signed to his label.

The success of Shady Records has allowed Eminem to expand his influence within the music industry. The label has given him a platform to shape the careers of other artists and influence the direction of hip-hop beyond his own music.

Shady Records has also served as a vehicle for Eminem to support and promote Detroit's hip-hop scene. By signing local artists and maintaining strong ties to the city's music community, Eminem has helped to keep Detroit on the map as a major hub of hip-hop talent.

The label's commitment to artist development sets it apart in an industry often focused on quick hits. Shady Records has shown a willingness to invest time and resources into nurturing talent, even when immediate commercial success isn't guaranteed.

Eminem's business ventures in music production have extended beyond Shady Records. He has worked on numerous film and television soundtracks, further diversifying his portfolio in the entertainment industry.

The establishment of Shady Records has also provided opportunities for Eminem to mentor younger artists. Many of the label's signees have spoken about the value of Eminem's guidance, both in terms of their artistic development and in navigating the music industry.

Shady Records' legacy in hip-hop is significant. The label has played a role in launching and supporting the careers of several important artists, contributing to the evolution of the genre over the past two decades.

Eminem's success with Shady Records has inspired other artists to launch their own labels. His model of artist-led record companies has become increasingly common in hip-hop, with many established rappers following in his footsteps.

12.2 Mom's Spaghetti Restaurant

Eminem's venture into the restaurant business with "Mom's Spaghetti" represents an innovative fusion of his artistic persona and entrepreneurial spirit. The concept, which takes its name from a famous line in his hit song "Lose Yourself," has grown from a clever pop-up idea to a permanent fixture in Detroit's culinary scene.

The origins of Mom's Spaghetti can be traced back to 2017, when Eminem and his team launched a pop-up restaurant in Detroit to coincide with the release of his album "Revival." The initial concept was met with enthusiasm from fans, who lined up for hours to taste spaghetti inspired by Eminem's lyrics.

Following the success of the pop-up, Mom's Spaghetti appeared at several music festivals, including Coachella in 2018. These appearances helped to build buzz around the concept and demonstrated its appeal beyond Detroit.

The decision to turn Mom's Spaghetti into a permanent restaurant came in 2021. Eminem and his business partners saw an opportunity to create a unique dining experience that would attract both fans and food enthusiasts.

Located in downtown Detroit, the permanent Mom's Spaghetti restau-

CHAPTER 12

rant opened its doors on September 29, 2021. The location, chosen for its proximity to Little Caesars Arena, strategically places the restaurant in a high-traffic area frequented by concert-goers and sports fans.

The menu at Mom's Spaghetti is intentionally simple, focusing on variations of spaghetti dishes. This streamlined approach not only references the song lyrics but also allows for efficient service and consistent quality.

One of the most popular items on the menu is the "s'ghetti sandwich," a novel creation that places spaghetti between two slices of garlic bread. This unique dish has become a signature item, embodying the playful and unconventional spirit of the restaurant.

The restaurant's design incorporates elements of Eminem's persona and Detroit's industrial aesthetic. The interior features a walk-up window styled to look like a Detroit trailer home, a nod to Eminem's roots and the city's working-class heritage.

Mom's Spaghetti has become more than just a restaurant; it's a destination for Eminem fans. Many visitors see eating there as a form of pilgrimage, a way to connect with the artist's music and story in a tangible way.

The success of Mom's Spaghetti has led to expansion plans. There have been discussions about opening locations in other cities, potentially turning the concept into a national or even international brand.

The restaurant has also ventured into merchandising, selling branded apparel and accessories. This move transforms Mom's Spaghetti from a mere eatery into a lifestyle brand associated with Eminem's image and music.

Eminem's involvement in the restaurant goes beyond lending his name. He has been hands-on in the development of the concept and menu, ensuring that it authentically represents his vision and maintains a connection to his artistry.

Mom's Spaghetti has received significant media attention, benefiting from Eminem's celebrity status. This publicity has helped to establish the restaurant as a must-visit destination in Detroit, attracting both locals and tourists.

The restaurant has also engaged in community initiatives, including partnerships with local charities and participation in Detroit's restaurant week. These efforts help to integrate Mom's Spaghetti into the fabric of the city's community.

The success of Mom's Spaghetti demonstrates Eminem's ability to leverage his personal brand in ventures outside of music. It shows his understanding of fan engagement and his capacity to transform elements of his artistic persona into successful business opportunities.

12.3 The Marshall Mathers Foundation and Charitable Work

Eminem's philanthropic efforts, primarily channeled through The Marshall Mathers Foundation, reflect a deep commitment to giving back to his community and supporting causes close to his heart. Established in 2005, the foundation has become a significant vehicle for Eminem's charitable work, focusing on disadvantaged youth in Detroit and its surrounding communities.

The foundation's primary mission is to provide assistance to organizations working with at-risk youth in Detroit and other areas of Michigan. This focus reflects Eminem's personal connection to the struggles faced by young people in urban environments, drawing from his own experiences growing up in Detroit.

One of the key areas of support for The Marshall Mathers Foundation is education. The foundation has provided funding for educational programs, scholarships, and school supplies, recognizing the importance of education in breaking the cycle of poverty.

The foundation has also been active in supporting programs that provide food and shelter to homeless and at-risk youth. These initiatives address immediate needs while also working towards long-term solutions to youth homelessness and food insecurity.

Eminem's foundation has shown a particular interest in supporting music and arts programs for young people. By funding these programs, the foundation helps to provide creative outlets and opportunities for self-expression to youth who might otherwise lack access to such resources.

The Marshall Mathers Foundation has partnered with various local and national organizations to maximize its impact. These collaborations have allowed the foundation to leverage its resources and reach a wider audience with its charitable efforts.

In addition to its ongoing programs, the foundation has responded to specific crises and emergencies. For example, during the Flint water crisis, Eminem and the foundation partnered with other organizations to provide bottled water and raise awareness about the issue.

Eminem's charitable work extends beyond the foundation. He has been known to make personal donations and participate in benefit concerts and events. These actions demonstrate his commitment to using his platform and resources for positive change.

The rapper's involvement in charity work has often been low-key, with many of his contributions made without fanfare or publicity. This approach reflects a genuine desire to help rather than a quest for positive PR.

Eminem's philanthropic efforts have also included support for addiction recovery programs. Given his own struggles with substance abuse, this is a cause that holds personal significance for him and allows him to make a meaningful impact in an area he understands intimately.

The foundation has supported initiatives aimed at promoting literacy among children and young adults. This focus aligns with Eminem's own love of wordplay and recognition of the power of language, seeking to inspire a similar passion in younger generations.

Through The Marshall Mathers Foundation, Eminem has also supported veterans' organizations. This support demonstrates a respect for service members and a recognition of the challenges many face upon returning to civilian life.

The foundation's work in Detroit has contributed to efforts to revitalize the city. By supporting local organizations and initiatives, Eminem is playing a role in the ongoing renaissance of his hometown.

Eminem's charitable work has inspired fan-led initiatives. Groups of fans have organized their own fundraising efforts in his name, extending the impact of his philanthropic example.

The Marshall Mathers Foundation has also supported health-related causes, including funding for children's hospitals and research into diseases affecting young people. This support reflects a holistic approach to improving the lives of youth in need.

Eminem's philanthropy has set an example for other artists in the hip-hop community. His commitment to giving back has encouraged other rappers to establish their own foundations and engage in charitable work.

The foundation's efforts have earned recognition from various charitable organizations and civic leaders. This acknowledgment has helped to highlight the positive impact that celebrities can have when they engage seriously in philanthropic work.

Eminem has used his music and platform to raise awareness about the causes supported by his foundation. Songs that touch on social issues often align with the foundation's mission, creating a synergy between his art and his charitable work.

The Marshall Mathers Foundation's work represents a significant aspect of Eminem's legacy, demonstrating that his impact extends far beyond his music. Through these efforts, he is working to create positive change in the communities that shaped him, giving back in meaningful and lasting ways.

CHAPTER 13

Legacy and Cultural Impact

13.1 Influence on Hip-Hop and Pop Culture

Eminem's influence on hip-hop and pop culture extends far beyond his record sales and accolades. His impact has reshaped the landscape of popular music, pushing boundaries and challenging conventions in ways that continue to reverberate through the industry.

The rapper's ability to bridge the gap between underground hip-hop and mainstream pop has been instrumental in bringing rap music to a wider audience. His crossover appeal opened doors for hip-hop to dominate popular culture in ways previously unseen, paving the way for future artists to achieve similar mainstream success.

Eminem's lyrical content, often controversial and always provocative, forced public discussions on topics that were previously taboo in mainstream discourse. His willingness to tackle subjects like domestic violence, drug addiction, and dysfunctional family dynamics brought these issues into the spotlight, challenging listeners and critics alike to confront uncomfortable truths.

The artist's unique style and image have had a lasting impact on fashion and popular aesthetics. The bleached blonde hair, white tank top, and baggy jeans became iconic, influencing countless imitators and leaving an indelible mark on early 2000s fashion trends.

Eminem's success paved the way for a new generation of rappers who didn't fit the traditional mold of hip-hop artists. His rise to fame demonstrated that authenticity and skill could transcend preconceived notions about who could succeed in the genre, inspiring diverse voices to make their mark in rap music.

The rapper's influence extends to language itself, with many of his lyrics and catchphrases entering the popular lexicon. Terms like "stan" have taken on lives of their own, becoming widely used in contexts far removed from their original source.

Eminem's impact on music videos cannot be overstated. His visually striking and often controversial videos pushed the boundaries of the medium, blending shock value with artistic expression in ways that influenced countless other artists.

The artist's success has had a profound impact on Detroit's cultural landscape. His continued association with the city has helped to keep Detroit in the cultural conversation, influencing perceptions of the city and its artistic output.

CHAPTER 13

Eminem's battles with other rappers, both on and off record, have become the stuff of hip-hop legend. These lyrical feuds have not only entertained fans but have also raised the bar for battle rap and diss tracks, influencing how artists engage in musical confrontations.

The rapper's candid discussions of his personal struggles, particularly his battles with addiction, have helped to destigmatize mental health issues within hip-hop culture. His openness has encouraged other artists to speak more freely about their own challenges.

Eminem's success has had a significant impact on the business side of the music industry. His ability to consistently sell albums in an era of declining physical sales has forced the industry to reevaluate its strategies and expectations.

The artist's collaborations with pop stars have helped to blur the lines between genres, contributing to the increasingly fluid nature of modern popular music. These crossover hits have expanded the possibilities for what hip-hop can sound like and who it can reach.

Eminem's influence can be seen in the technical aspects of rapping as well. His complex rhyme schemes and rapid-fire delivery have set new standards for lyrical proficiency, inspiring countless artists to push their technical skills to new heights.

The rapper's alter ego, Slim Shady, has become a cultural icon in its own right. This persona has influenced how other artists approach character creation and storytelling in their music, expanding the narrative possibilities within hip-hop.

Eminem's impact on popular culture extends to film and television, where his music and persona have been referenced, parodied, and celebrated countless times. These appearances in various media have cemented his status as a pop culture icon beyond just the world of music.

13.2 Breaking Racial Barriers in Rap

Eminem's rise to prominence in hip-hop marked a significant shift in the genre's racial dynamics. His success as a white rapper in a predominantly black art form challenged long-held assumptions about race and authenticity in hip-hop, paving the way for greater diversity within the genre.

The artist's early career was marked by skepticism and resistance from some quarters of the hip-hop community. Eminem had to prove himself repeatedly, facing challenges and prejudices that tested his commitment to the art form. His ability to overcome these obstacles demonstrated that skill and passion could transcend racial barriers.

Eminem's partnership with Dr. Dre played a crucial role in his acceptance within the hip-hop community. Dre's cosign lent Eminem credibility and opened doors that might otherwise have remained closed to a white rapper. This collaboration challenged preconceptions about racial collaboration in hip-hop.

The rapper's lyrical content often directly addressed issues of race and his position as a white artist in a black genre. Songs like "White America" tackled these themes head-on, forcing listeners to confront their own prejudices and assumptions about race in music.

Eminem's success inspired a new generation of white rappers, demonstrating that there was a place for them in hip-hop if they approached the genre with respect and skill. However, this also led to debates about cultural appropriation and the responsibilities of white artists in black spaces.

The artist's rise coincided with hip-hop's growing mainstream appeal, and he played a significant role in bringing the genre to white suburban audiences. This expanded reach had both positive and negative consequences, broadening hip-hop's influence while also raising concerns about the dilution of its cultural roots.

Eminem's technical skill as a rapper challenged racist assumptions about who could excel in hip-hop. His complex rhyme schemes and rapid-fire delivery set new standards for lyricism, proving that mastery of the art form was not confined to any one racial group.

The rapper's exploration of his own whiteness and its implications in his music added new dimensions to hip-hop's discourse on race. His willingness to engage with these issues openly and honestly contributed to more nuanced conversations about race within and beyond the genre.

Eminem's success opened doors for collaborations between white and black artists in hip-hop that might not have been possible before. These partnerships helped to break down racial barriers and foster a more inclusive hip-hop community.

The artist's impact extended beyond just music, influencing broader cultural conversations about race and identity. His prominence forced media and critics to reevaluate their understanding of hip-hop and its place in American culture.

Eminem's journey in hip-hop highlighted the complexities of racial dynamics in American popular culture. His story became a focal point for discussions about privilege, authenticity, and the evolving nature of cultural ownership in music.

The rapper's success challenged the music industry's traditional marketing categories, forcing a reconsideration of how artists are promoted and to whom. This shift had far-reaching implications for how race is considered in music marketing and promotion.

Eminem's rise also sparked debates about the future of hip-hop as a genre. Some feared that his success would lead to a whitewashing of the art form, while others saw it as an opportunity for hip-hop to evolve and reach new audiences without losing its core identity.

The artist's acknowledgment of his privilege as a white rapper in a black genre set an important precedent. His willingness to engage with these issues thoughtfully demonstrated a path for other white artists to participate in hip-hop culture responsibly.

Eminem's breaking of racial barriers in rap has had a lasting impact on the genre. Today, hip-hop is more diverse than ever, with artists from various racial and cultural backgrounds contributing to its evolution. This diversity, while not solely attributable to Eminem, was certainly accelerated by his groundbreaking career.

13.3 Impact on Lyricism and Wordplay

Eminem's impact on lyricism and wordplay in hip-hop is profound and far-reaching. His innovative approach to rhyme schemes, syllable patterns, and narrative structures has raised the bar for technical proficiency in rap, influencing a generation of artists and redefining what's possible within the confines of a verse.

The rapper's complex rhyme schemes, often featuring multi-syllabic rhymes and internal rhyming, have become a benchmark for lyrical complexity in hip-hop. His ability to string together long sequences of rhyming words and phrases has challenged other artists to push their own boundaries.

Eminem's use of assonance and consonance has added new dimensions to hip-hop lyricism. His careful attention to the sounds of words, not just their meanings, has created a more musical approach to rapping that has influenced countless artists.

The artist's storytelling abilities have expanded the narrative possibilities within rap. Songs like "Stan" demonstrated how a rap song could tell a complex, nuanced story, complete with character development and plot twists, all within the constraints of rhyme and rhythm.

Eminem's wordplay often incorporates clever puns and double entendres, adding layers of meaning to his lyrics. This approach has encouraged listeners and fellow artists to pay closer attention to the intricacies of language in rap music.

The rapper's use of alter egos, particularly Slim Shady, has influenced how other artists approach character creation and perspective in their lyrics. This technique has opened up new avenues for storytelling and self-expression in The rapper's use of alter egos, particularly Slim Shady, has influenced how other artists approach character creation and perspective in their lyrics. This technique has opened up new avenues for storytelling and self-expression in hip-hop, allowing artists to explore different facets of their personalities and experiences.

Eminem's rapid-fire delivery style has pushed the boundaries of what's technically possible in rap. His ability to fit complex thoughts and intricate rhyme schemes into tight spaces has inspired other rappers to increase their own verbal dexterity.

The artist's clever use of pop culture references has become a hallmark of his style, influencing how other rappers incorporate cultural touchstones into their lyrics. This approach has made hip-hop lyrics a rich tapestry of contemporary references, rewarding close listening and cultural awareness.

Eminem's willingness to play with language, including the creation of new words and the creative misuse of existing ones, has expanded the vocabulary of hip-hop. His linguistic innovations have often found their way into popular speech, demonstrating the power of rap to influence language itself.

The rapper's use of shock value in his lyrics, while controversial, has pushed the boundaries of what can be said in popular music. This has led to broader discussions about freedom of expression and the role of provocative art in society.

Eminem's technical prowess has raised the standard for what constitutes skillful rapping. His influence can be seen in the increasing emphasis on complex lyricism in hip-hop, with many artists striving to demonstrate similar levels of verbal acrobatics.

The artist's approach to rhythm and flow, often switching up his cadence multiple times within a single verse, has influenced how rappers think about the musicality of their delivery. This has led to more dynamic and unpredictable flows in hip-hop.

Eminem's lyrics often feature a stream-of-consciousness style that allows for rapid transitions between ideas and images. This approach has influenced other artists to experiment with more free-associative and surreal lyrical techniques.

The rapper's use of humor in his lyrics, ranging from crude jokes to sophisticated wordplay, has demonstrated how comedy can be effectively integrated into serious artistic expression. This has encouraged other artists to incorporate more humor into their work.

Eminem's detailed, confessional style of songwriting has influenced how personal rappers are willing to be in their lyrics. His openness about his struggles and flaws has paved the way for more vulnerable and introspective approaches to hip-hop lyricism.

The artist's skill at crafting memorable hooks and choruses, often incorporating complex rhymes and wordplay, has raised the bar for what's expected in hip-hop songwriting. This has led to a greater emphasis on crafting every part of a song, not just the verses.

Eminem's battles and diss tracks have set new standards for lyrical combat in hip-hop. His attention to detail, personal jabs, and technical flourishes in these confrontational pieces have influenced how rappers approach musical feuds.

The rapper's use of extended metaphors and analogies has demonstrated how complex ideas can be explored through figurative language in hip-hop. This has encouraged more ambitious and abstract lyricism in the genre.

Eminem's influence extends to the way rappers structure their verses and albums. His use of conceptual continuity, callbacks, and overarching narratives has inspired more cohesive and thematically rich approaches to hip-hop songwriting and album crafting.

The artist's impact on lyricism and wordplay in hip-hop cannot be overstated. His technical innovations, storytelling prowess, and willingness to push boundaries have left an indelible mark on the genre, influencing artists across multiple generations and continually raising the bar for what's possible in rap lyricism.

CHAPTER 14

Personal Life and Family

14.1 Relationship with Daughter Hailie

Eminem's relationship with his daughter Hailie Jade Scott has been a central theme throughout his career, often serving as both inspiration for his music and a grounding force in his personal life. Born on December 25, 1995, Hailie has been a constant presence in Eminem's lyrics, with numerous songs dedicated to or mentioning her.

The rapper's devotion to his daughter is evident in tracks like "Hailie's Song" from "The Eminem Show," where he expresses his love and the positive impact she has had on his life. This song, in particular, offers a rare glimpse into Eminem's softer side, contrasting sharply with his often confrontational public persona.

Eminem's efforts to shield Hailie from the negative aspects of his fame have been well-documented. He has consistently worked to provide her with a sense of normalcy, despite the extraordinary circumstances of being the child of one of the world's most famous musicians. This commitment to her well-being has often meant keeping her out of the public eye.

The challenges of balancing his career with fatherhood have been a recurring theme in Eminem's music. Songs like "Mockingbird" address the difficulties he faced in being present for Hailie while dealing with the demands of his rapidly rising fame and his tumultuous relationship with her mother, Kim Scott.

Hailie's presence in Eminem's life has been credited by the rapper as a stabilizing force, particularly during his struggles with addiction. In interviews, he has spoken about how the desire to be a good father to Hailie motivated him to overcome his substance abuse issues and focus on his recovery.

The evolution of Eminem's relationship with Hailie can be traced through his discography. Early tracks often express anxiety about his ability to provide for her and protect her, while later songs reflect a more mature perspective on fatherhood and his growing confidence in his parental role.

Eminem's commitment to Hailie's education has been notable. He has spoken proudly of her academic achievements, including her graduation from Michigan State University. This emphasis on education reflects his desire for her to have opportunities that were not available to him in his youth.

The rapper's protectiveness towards Hailie has extended to his music, where he has often lashed out at media figures or other celebrities who have mentioned her name. This fierce defense of his daughter's privacy underscores the importance he places on keeping her life separate from his public persona.

Hailie's occasional public appearances and social media presence in recent years have garnered significant attention, highlighting the ongoing public fascination with Eminem's family life. However, both father and daughter have maintained a level of discretion about their relationship, keeping many aspects of their bond private.

Eminem's role as a father has undoubtedly influenced his artistic output, adding depth and emotional resonance to his work. The vulnerability he displays when discussing Hailie in his music offers listeners a more complete picture of the man behind the controversial public figure.

The rapper's dedication to co-parenting with Kim Scott, despite their tumultuous history, demonstrates his commitment to providing a stable family environment for Hailie. This aspect of his personal life has been less publicized but is crucial to understanding his priorities as a father.

Hailie's influence on Eminem extends beyond just inspiring his music. Her presence in his life has been a humanizing factor, allowing fans and critics alike to see a more relatable side of the often-polarizing artist. This has contributed to a more nuanced public perception of Eminem over the years.

The growing public interest in Hailie as she has entered adulthood presents new challenges for Eminem in terms of maintaining her privacy while supporting her independence. His navigation of this complex situation continues to evolve, reflecting the ongoing nature of their father-daughter relationship.

Eminem's relationship with Hailie serves as a powerful counterpoint to the more controversial aspects of his public persona. It highlights the complexity of his character and the importance he places on family, adding depth to the public's understanding of one of hip-hop's most influential figures.

The enduring nature of Eminem's bond with Hailie, spanning over two decades of his career, stands as a testament to the central role she plays in his life. It remains a defining aspect of his personal narrative, continuing to influence both his music and his public image.

14.2 Adopting Other Family Members

Eminem's family dynamics extend beyond his relationship with his biological daughter Hailie, encompassing the adoption and care of other family members. This aspect of his personal life demonstrates a commitment to family that goes beyond traditional boundaries, reflecting a broader definition of parental responsibility.

The rapper's decision to adopt his niece Alaina Marie Mathers (born Amanda Marie Scott) showcases his willingness to step into a parental role for children in need within his extended family. Alaina, the daughter of Kim Scott's twin sister Dawn, was born in 1993 and was adopted by Eminem in the mid-2000s.

Eminem's adoption of Alaina was motivated by a desire to provide stability and opportunity in the face of challenging family circumstances. This decision reflects his understanding of the impact a troubled upbringing can have on a child, drawing from his own experiences growing up in Detroit.

The rapper's lyrics occasionally reference Alaina, often referring to her as Lainie. These mentions, while less frequent than those of Hailie, demonstrate that she is an integral part of his family unit. Songs like "Going Through Changes" include lines that express his love and commitment to both Hailie and Alaina equally.

Eminem's role in Alaina's life extends beyond legal adoption. He has taken on the full responsibilities of fatherhood, including providing for her education and shielding her from the potential negative impacts of his fame. This commitment mirrors his approach to raising Hailie.

The inclusion of Alaina in Eminem's family has added another dimension to his public persona. It showcases a nurturing side that contrasts with his often-aggressive artistic image, offering a more complete picture of his character to fans and critics alike.

Eminem's adoption of Alaina also highlights his awareness of the importance of family support systems. By stepping in to care for his niece, he demonstrates an understanding of the broader responsibilities that come with being part of an extended family network.

The rapper's experience with adoption has likely influenced his perspective on family and parenting. This expanded view of family is reflected in his music and public statements, where he often emphasizes the importance of being there for loved ones, regardless of biological connections.

Eminem's decision to adopt Alaina has had a ripple effect, influencing public perceptions of adoption and non-traditional family structures. His high-profile example serves to normalize and celebrate diverse family compositions.

The challenges of raising an adopted child in the public eye are considerable, and Eminem's efforts to protect Alaina's privacy mirror his approach with Hailie. This consistent stance on family privacy underscores his priorities as a parent, famous or not.

Eminem's role as an adoptive father to Alaina has also likely influenced his philanthropic efforts. His foundation's focus on assisting disadvantaged youth may well be informed by his personal experiences in expanding his family through adoption.

The rapper's commitment to Alaina extends to ensuring equity among his children. In interviews and through his actions, Eminem has made it clear that he makes no distinction between his biological and adopted children in terms of love, support, or provision.

Eminem's adoption of Alaina serves as a powerful example of taking responsibility for family members in need. This action speaks to his character beyond his musical talent, highlighting a sense of duty and compassion that may surprise those who know him only through his often-controversial public persona.

The inclusion of Alaina in Eminem's family narrative adds depth to the personal stories that inform his music. While he maintains a level of privacy around his children, the knowledge of his expanded family role provides context for the emotional depth found in much of his work.

Eminem's experience as an adoptive father to Alaina, combined with his relationship with Hailie, paints a picture of a man deeply committed to family. This aspect of his life stands as a significant counterpoint to the more turbulent elements of his public image, offering a more nuanced understanding of one of hip-hop's most complex figures.

14.3 Balancing Fame and Privacy

Eminem's journey through fame has been marked by a constant struggle to balance his public persona with his desire for personal privacy. This tension between his high-profile career and his need for a private life has been a defining aspect of his personal narrative.

The rapper's rise to superstardom in the late 1990s and early 2000s thrust him into a level of public scrutiny that few artists experience. Paparazzi, tabloids, and obsessive fans created an environment where every aspect of his life became potential fodder for public consumption.

Eminem's approach to managing this intense public interest has evolved over time. In the early years of his fame, he often used his music and public appearances to directly confront and challenge those who invaded his privacy. Songs like "The Way I Am" expressed his frustration with constant media attention and fan obsession.

The artist's efforts to protect his daughter Hailie from the negative aspects of his fame have been particularly notable. He has consistently worked to keep her out of the public eye, rarely allowing her to be photographed or interviewed. This protective stance extends to his other family members as well.

Eminem's retreat from the public eye during his struggles with addiction and subsequent recovery period demonstrated his willingness to prioritize his personal well-being over his public image. This hiatus allowed him to focus on his health and family away from the glare of media attention.

The rapper's selective use of social media and limited public appearances in recent years reflect a carefully managed approach to fame. By controlling the flow of information about his personal life, Eminem has created a buffer between his public persona and his private world.

Eminem's lyrics often serve as a window into his personal life, but he maintains control over what is revealed through his music. This artistic outlet allows him to share personal experiences on his own terms, providing a sense of authenticity without fully compromising his privacy.

The artist's decision to live primarily in Michigan, away from entertainment hubs like Los Angeles or New York, is part of his strategy to maintain a semblance of normal life. This geographic distance provides a physical barrier between his home life and the center of the entertainment industry.

Eminem's interactions with fans have been carefully managed to maintain boundaries. While he expresses appreciation for his fan base, he rarely engages in activities that would allow for invasive access to his personal life, such as meet-and-greets or extensive social media interactions.

The rapper's legal team has played a crucial role in protecting his privacy, taking action against those who cross the line into invasion of privacy or defamation. This proactive approach has helped to establish clear boundaries around what is considered acceptable coverage of his personal life.

Eminem's relationships, particularly his on-again, off-again marriage to Kim Scott, have been subject to intense public scrutiny. His approach to discussing these personal matters has typically been to address them through his music rather than through interviews or public statements, allowing him to control the narrative.

The artist's ability to separate his stage persona from his private self has been crucial in maintaining his personal life. While Slim Shady may be outrageous and confrontational, Marshall Mathers can retreat to a more grounded existence away from the spotlight.

Eminem's privacy efforts extend to his business dealings and philanthropic work. Many of his charitable contributions are made anonymously or with minimal publicity, reflecting a desire to do good without seeking public acclaim.

The rapper's approach to fame and privacy has influenced other artists in the hip-hop community and beyond. His ability to maintain a level of mystique while still connecting with fans through his art has become a model for celebrities seeking to protect their personal lives.

Eminem's balancing act between fame and privacy remains an ongoing process. As the media landscape evolves, with social media creating new challenges for personal privacy, the rapper continues to adapt his strategies to protect his personal sphere while maintaining his artistic relevance.

15

Conclusion

Eminem's Ongoing Career and Future

Recent Albums and Musical Evolution

Eminem's recent albums showcase an artist continuously evolving, adapting to the changing landscape of hip-hop while maintaining the core elements that have defined his career. His releases in the past decade demonstrate a willingness to experiment with new styles and themes, reflecting his growth both as an artist and as a person.

"Revival," released in 2017, marked a departure from Eminem's earlier sound. The album featured more pop-oriented production and collaborations with mainstream artists, signaling an attempt to broaden his appeal. While receiving mixed reviews, "Revival" highlighted Eminem's ability to tackle political and social issues, particularly in tracks like "Untouchable" and "Like Home."

CONCLUSION

The surprise release of "Kamikaze" in 2018 saw Eminem return to a more aggressive, confrontational style. This album was widely seen as a response to the criticism of "Revival," with Eminem taking aim at his detractors and reasserting his position in the rap game. The rapid-fire delivery and complex wordplay on tracks like "The Ringer" and "Lucky You" reminded listeners of Eminem's technical prowess.

"Music to Be Murdered By," released in 2020, and its companion piece "Music to Be Murdered By – Side B," released later the same year, further showcased Eminem's versatility. These albums blended elements of his earlier work with more mature reflections on his life and career. Tracks like "Darkness" demonstrated his continued ability to craft narratives that engage with complex social issues.

Throughout these recent releases, Eminem has shown a willingness to collaborate with a diverse array of artists, from pop stars to up-and-coming rappers. These collaborations have allowed him to explore new sounds and styles, keeping his music fresh and relevant to younger audiences.

Eminem's lyrical content in recent years has evolved to include more introspective and socially conscious themes. While still maintaining his trademark wordplay and occasional shock value, he has increasingly used his platform to address issues such as gun violence, racial inequality, and mental health.

The production on Eminem's recent albums reflects a balance between honoring his roots and embracing contemporary sounds. He has worked with a mix of long-time collaborators and new producers, resulting in a sound that bridges different eras of hip-hop.

Eminem's vocal delivery has also evolved in his recent work. While still capable of the rapid-fire flows that made him famous, he has also experimented with more melodic approaches and varied cadences, demonstrating his adaptability as a vocalist.

These recent albums have shown Eminem grappling with his legacy and place in the hip-hop pantheon. Tracks like "Walk On Water" and "Leaving Heaven" reveal an artist reflecting on his impact and the pressures of maintaining his status in the rap world.

Eminem's willingness to address his past controversies and personal growth in his recent music adds depth to his discography. This self-awareness and maturity have allowed him to maintain his artistic integrity while evolving with the times.

The critical and commercial reception of these recent albums has been varied, but they have all sparked significant discussion within the hip-hop community and beyond. This ongoing engagement with Eminem's work underscores his continued relevance and influence in the music industry.

Eminem's recent musical output demonstrates an artist who refuses to rest on his laurels. By continuing to challenge himself and his audience, he ensures that each new release is an event in the hip-hop world, eagerly anticipated and intensely debated.

CONCLUSION

Continued Relevance in the Rap Scene

Eminem's continued relevance in the rap scene is a testament to his enduring impact on the genre and his ability to adapt to its evolving landscape. Decades after his breakthrough, he remains a significant figure in hip-hop, influencing new generations of artists and contributing to ongoing conversations within the culture.

His technical skills continue to set a high bar for lyricism in rap. Eminem's complex rhyme schemes, wordplay, and rapid-fire delivery are still regarded as benchmarks of excellence in hip-hop, inspiring younger artists to push their own boundaries.

Eminem's willingness to engage with and mentor emerging talents has helped maintain his connection to the contemporary rap scene. His collaborations with artists like Juice WRLD, Joyner Lucas, and others have bridged generational gaps in hip-hop.

His influence extends beyond his own music, with many current rap stars citing him as a major inspiration. This acknowledgment from newer artists helps to cement Eminem's legacy and ensures his continued relevance in discussions about hip-hop's greatest contributors.

Eminem's ability to generate controversy and spark debate remains undiminished. His provocative lyrics and willingness to tackle sensitive subjects continue to make him a lightning rod for discussion, keeping him at the forefront of cultural conversations.

His performances at major events and award shows consistently draw attention and acclaim. Eminem's appearance at the 2020 Academy Awards, where he performed "Lose Yourself" 17 years after its Oscar win, demonstrated his enduring star power and ability to captivate audiences.

Eminem's record-breaking achievements continue to make headlines. His ability to top charts and break streaming records with new releases speaks to his ongoing popularity and cultural significance.

His influence on hip-hop extends to the business side of the industry. Through Shady Records, Eminem continues to shape the careers of other artists and influence the direction of rap music.

Eminem's willingness to address current events and social issues in his music keeps him relevant to contemporary audiences. His engagement with topics like political divisiveness, racial tensions, and the COVID-19 pandemic in recent tracks demonstrates his commitment to using his platform to comment on the world around him.

His longevity in a genre often associated with youth culture is noteworthy. Eminem's ability to maintain his relevance well into his 40s challenges preconceptions about age in hip-hop and sets a precedent for career longevity in the genre.

Eminem's impact on popular culture extends beyond music. His influence can be seen in film, television, and broader cultural discourse, cementing his status as not just a rap icon, but a pop culture phenomenon.

His ongoing feuds and lyrical battles with other rappers continue to generate interest and excitement within the hip-hop community. These exchanges demonstrate Eminem's continued engagement with the competitive aspects of rap culture.

CONCLUSION

Eminem's ability to surprise audiences with unexpected releases and collaborations keeps fans and critics alike on their toes. This unpredictability helps maintain a sense of excitement and anticipation around his work.

His continued commercial success in an era of declining album sales is remarkable. Eminem's ability to adapt to new distribution models while still moving significant units speaks to his enduring appeal and business acumen.

Eminem's relevance is also maintained through his influence on language and popular expression. Terms and phrases from his lyrics continue to permeate popular culture, demonstrating the lasting impact of his wordcraft.

Future Projects and Artistic Direction

Eminem's future projects and artistic direction remain subjects of intense speculation and interest within the music industry and among his fanbase. While the rapper has always been notoriously secretive about his upcoming work, certain trends and hints suggest possible paths for his artistic journey.

"The Death of Slim Shady (Coup de Grâce)" hints at potential new directions for Eminem's artistry. The album's concept of battling his alter ego suggests a period of introspection and possibly a new artistic phase.

Eminem's future work may involve deeper exploration of socially conscious themes, building on the political and social commentary present in his recent albums. His engagement with current events and societal issues in "The Death of Slim Shady (Coup de Grâce)" indicates a growing commitment to using his platform for meaningful commentary.

The possibility of further experimentation with different sub-genres of hip-hop and even ventures into other musical styles remains open. Eminem's recent collaborations with artists from various genres suggest a continued interest in pushing the boundaries of his sound.

There is potential for Eminem to delve deeper into socially conscious themes in his future work. His recent engagement with political and social issues indicates a growing commitment to using his platform for commentary on pressing societal concerns.

The concept of legacy and reflection on his career may play a significant role in Eminem's future projects. As he enters the later stages of his career, themes of nostalgia, impact, and artistic heritage could become more prominent in his lyrics.

Collaborations with both established legends and emerging talents in hip-hop are likely to feature in Eminem's future work. These partnerships could serve to both honor his roots and maintain his connection to the evolving rap landscape.

The potential for a concept album or a project that significantly departs from his established style remains an intriguing possibility. Eminem's artistic restlessness and desire to challenge himself could lead to unexpected creative directions.

Further exploration of personal themes, particularly his experiences as

CONCLUSION

he ages and his perspective on his tumultuous life journey, may inform his future artistic output. This could result in more introspective and reflective material.

The possibility of Eminem taking on more production work, both for himself and other artists, could shape his future in the industry. His growing experience behind the boards may lead to a more hands-on approach in crafting his sound.

Eminem's future projects might include more multimedia elements, potentially incorporating visual albums, extended music videos, or even forays into film and television production. His experience with "8 Mile" and various music videos suggests an interest in visual storytelling.

The rapper's commitment to technical excellence in his craft suggests that future projects will continue to showcase complex lyricism and innovative wordplay. This dedication to the fundamentals of MCing is likely to remain a cornerstone of his artistic direction.

Eminem's future work may involve more direct mentorship of younger artists, potentially through collaborative albums or projects that showcase emerging talent. This could serve as a way to solidify his legacy while contributing to the future of hip-hop.

The possibility of a farewell album or a final tour remains a topic of speculation. While Eminem has not indicated any plans to retire, the concept of how a hip-hop legend concludes their career could be an intriguing artistic challenge for him to tackle.

Future projects might see Eminem exploring more vulnerable or personal topics that he has previously kept private. As he matures as an artist and a person, there may be a desire to share more intimate aspects of his life and thoughts through his music.

The potential for Eminem to revisit and reimagine earlier works or characters from his discography could provide an interesting artistic direction. This could involve updating older concepts or providing new perspectives on familiar themes.

Eminem's future artistic direction may involve more live instrumentation or orchestral elements, building on experiments in this direction from his recent albums. This could lead to a richer, more layered sound in his productions.

The rapper's interest in battling and competitive aspects of hip-hop culture might influence future projects, potentially leading to more collaborative battle-style tracks or even organized lyrical competitions.

Eminem's future work could see him taking on more of an elder statesman role in hip-hop, offering commentary on the state of the genre and its evolution. This perspective could provide valuable insights into the changing landscape of rap music.

Conclusion:

Eminem's career stands as a testament to the power of raw talent, relentless determination, and unapologetic authenticity. From his humble beginnings in Detroit to his status as a global icon, he has redefined the boundaries of hip-hop and left an indelible mark on popular culture.

His journey through personal struggles, controversies, and artistic

CONCLUSION

triumphs has captivated audiences for decades. Eminem's ability to channel his experiences into compelling, often provocative music has established him as one of the most influential artists of his generation.

The evolution of his artistry, from the shock value of his early work to the more introspective and socially conscious themes of his recent albums, reflects a artist who has grown alongside his audience. His willingness to adapt and experiment while maintaining his core identity has ensured his continued relevance in a rapidly changing musical landscape.

Eminem's impact extends far beyond his own discography. He has broken racial barriers in hip-hop, inspired countless artists across genres, and pushed the technical boundaries of lyricism and wordplay. His influence can be heard in the work of many contemporary rappers and felt in the broader cultural conversations he has sparked.

As Eminem continues to navigate the later stages of his career, his legacy is already secure. He stands as a pivotal figure in the history of hip-hop, a controversial but undeniably talented artist who has shaped the genre and popular music as a whole. Whatever direction his future projects take, they will be met with the intense interest and scrutiny that has followed him throughout his remarkable career.

The story of Eminem is one of triumph over adversity, artistic integrity in the face of criticism, and the enduring power of self-expression. As he moves forward, his journey remains a compelling narrative of an artist who continues to challenge himself, his audience, and the very boundaries of his chosen art form.

Afterword

Eminem's journey through the world of hip-hop has been nothing short of extraordinary. From his humble beginnings in Detroit to becoming a global icon, his career has been marked by unprecedented success, controversy, and artistic evolution. This afterword serves to encapsulate the magnitude of his impact on music and popular culture, as well as provide a comprehensive overview of his achievements and discography.

The numbers alone speak volumes about Eminem's influence and popularity. With global sales exceeding 220 million records, he stands as one of the best-selling music artists in history. His dominance in the music industry is further evidenced by his reign as the bestselling music artist from 2000 to 2009 in the United States, according to Nielsen SoundScan. This success continued into the following decade, with Eminem claiming the title of bestselling male music artist in the United States for the 2010s.

Eminem's impact on the charts has been equally impressive. He has achieved thirteen number-one albums on the Billboard 200, a feat that includes nine solo efforts, two with D12, and one with Bad Meets Evil. His ability to consistently top the charts across multiple decades demonstrates not only his enduring popularity but also his ability to evolve and remain relevant in an ever-changing musical landscape.

AFTERWORD

The recognition of Eminem's talent and impact extends far beyond album sales. His trophy case boasts an impressive array of awards, including 15 Grammy Awards, eight American Music Awards, and 17 Billboard Music Awards. The diversity of these accolades speaks to his ability to appeal to both critics and popular audiences alike. Billboard's naming of Eminem as the "Artist of the Decade (2000-2009)" further solidifies his status as a defining figure in modern music.

Eminem's influence reaches beyond the realm of music. His performance in the semi-autobiographical film "8 Mile" earned him an Academy Award for Best Original Song for "Lose Yourself," making him the first rapper to receive this prestigious honor. This crossover success highlighted Eminem's versatility as an artist and his ability to translate his narrative skills to the big screen.

The rapper's technical prowess and artistic impact have been widely recognized by his peers and music critics. Rolling Stone included him in their lists of the 100 Greatest Artists of All Time and the 100 Greatest Songwriters of All Time, acknowledging both his performance skills and his songwriting abilities. MTV ranked him 9th on their Greatest MCs of All Time list, while The Source placed him 6th on their list of the Top 50 Lyricists of All Time.

Eminem's discography stands as a testament to his prolific output and artistic growth. His studio albums, from 1996's "Infinite" to 2020's "Music to Be Murdered By," chart the evolution of his style and themes. Each album represents a chapter in Eminem's life and career, reflecting his personal struggles, societal observations, and artistic experimentation.

The Slim Shady LP (1999) marked Eminem's major-label debut and introduced the world to his alter ego, Slim Shady. This album set the tone for his early career, showcasing his technical skills and controversial lyrics. The Marshall Mathers LP (2000) and The Eminem Show (2002) further cemented his status as a hip-hop icon, with both albums achieving Diamond certification from the RIAA.

Encore (2004) saw Eminem grappling with the pressures of fame and expectations, while Relapse (2009) marked his return after a hiatus and dealt with themes of addiction and recovery. Recovery (2010) represented a more introspective and mature Eminem, with the rapper exploring themes of personal growth and resilience.

The Marshall Mathers LP 2 (2013) revisited themes from earlier in his career but with the perspective of an older, more experienced artist. Revival (2017) and Kamikaze (2018) saw Eminem engaging with political themes and responding to critics, respectively. Music to Be Murdered By (2020) showcased his continued ability to surprise and provoke, blending his signature style with contemporary production.

Throughout his career, Eminem has also been a collaborative force in hip-hop. His work with D12 resulted in two successful albums, Devil's Night (2001) and D12 World (2004). His partnership with Royce da 5'9" as Bad Meets Evil produced Hell: The Sequel (2011), demonstrating his continued connection to his Detroit roots.

Eminem's tours have been equally impactful, allowing him to connect with fans around the world. From The Slim Shady LP Tour in 1999 to the Revival Tour in 2018, his live performances have been known for their energy, technical precision, and ability to bring his complex lyrics to life on stage.

The rapper's influence extends to the written word as well. His books, Angry Blonde (2000) and The Way I Am (2008), offered fans a deeper look into his creative process and personal life, further cementing his connection with his audience.

Eminem's career serves as a blueprint for longevity and evolution in hip-hop. His ability to maintain relevance and commercial success over multiple decades is a testament to his skill, work ethic, and willingness to grow as an artist. From the shock value of his early work to the more introspective and socially conscious themes of his later albums, Eminem has consistently pushed the boundaries of what rap music can be.

The legacy of Eminem is still being written. His impact on hip-hop, popular culture, and the music industry as a whole is undeniable. He has inspired countless artists, challenged societal norms, and redefined what it means to be a rapper. As he continues to create and evolve, Eminem's place in the pantheon of music legends is assured, his influence certain to be felt for generations to come.

Eminem's Awards and Discography

Awards and Honors:

- 15 Grammy Awards
- 8 American Music Awards

- 17 Billboard Music Awards
- Academy Award for Best Original Song ("Lose Yourself" - 2003)
- MTV Europe Music Awards Global Icon Award (2013)
- Billboard "Artist of the Decade" (2000-2009)
- Inducted into the Rock and Roll Hall of Fame (Class of 2022)

Notable Rankings:

- Rolling Stone: 100 Greatest Artists of All Time
- Rolling Stone: 100 Greatest Songwriters of All Time
- MTV: 9th Greatest MC of All Time
- The Source: 6th on Top 50 Lyricists of All Time

Discography:

Studio Albums:

1. Infinite (1996)
2. The Slim Shady LP (1999)
3. The Marshall Mathers LP (2000)
4. The Eminem Show (2002)
5. Encore (2004)
6. Relapse (2009)
7. Recovery (2010)
8. The Marshall Mathers LP 2 (2013)
9. Revival (2017)

10. Kamikaze (2018)
11. Music to Be Murdered By (2020)
12. The Death of Slim Shady (Coup de Grâce) (2024)

Collaborative Albums:

1. Devil's Night (with D12) (2001)
2. D12 World (with D12) (2004)
3. Eminem Presents: The Re-Up (with Shady Records) (2006)
4. Hell: The Sequel (with Bad Meets Evil) (2011)
5. Shady XV (with Shady Records) (2014)

Major Tours:

- The Slim Shady LP Tour (1999)
- Up in Smoke Tour (2000)
- Anger Management Tour (2002-2005)
- The Recovery Tour (2010-2013)
- The Monster Tour (with Rihanna) (2014)
- Revival Tour (2018)

Literary Works:

- Angry Blonde (2000)
- The Way I Am (2008)

Made in the USA
Monee, IL
19 February 2025